THE LOVES OF OUR LIVES

KARSYN WALLACE

NEW DEGREE PRESS

THE LOVES OF OUR LIVES

ISBN   978-1-63676-904-2   *Paperback*

              978-1-63676-968-4   *Kindle Ebook*

              978-1-63730-072-5   *Ebook*

For my family

CONTENTS

———

PART 1.   EMI   **9**

   CHAPTER ONE   11

   CHAPTER TWO   19

   CHAPTER THREE   27

   CHAPTER FOUR   33

   CHAPTER FIVE   39

   CHAPTER SIX   43

   CHAPTER SEVEN   47

   CHAPTER EIGHT   53

   CHAPTER NINE   57

   CHAPTER TEN   65

PART 2.   JO   **69**

   CHAPTER ELEVEN   71

   CHAPTER TWELVE   77

   CHAPTER THIRTEEN   83

   CHAPTER FOURTEEN   87

   CHAPTER FIFTEEN   97

   CHAPTER SIXTEEN   103

   CHAPTER SEVENTEEN   109

   CHAPTER EIGHTEEN   117

   CHAPTER NINETEEN   123

   CHAPTER TWENTY   129

   CHAPTER TWENTY-ONE   137

   CHAPTER TWENTY-TWO   141

PART 3.   **WILLA**   **147**

    CHAPTER TWENTY-THREE   149

    CHAPTER TWENTY-FOUR   157

    CHAPTER TWENTY-FIVE   165

    CHAPTER TWENTY-SIX   173

    CHAPTER TWENTY-SEVEN   181

    CHAPTER TWENTY-EIGHT   185

    CHAPTER TWENTY-NINE   189

    CHAPTER THIRTY   193

    CHAPTER THIRTY-ONE   199

    CHAPTER THIRTY-TWO   205

    CHAPTER THIRTY-THREE   209

PART 4.   **LOSING**   **213**

    CHAPTER THIRTY-FOUR: EMI   215

    CHAPTER THIRTY-FIVE: WILLA   221

    CHAPTER THIRTY-SIX: EMI   225

    CHAPTER THIRTY-SEVEN: WILLA   229

    CHAPTER THIRTY-EIGHT: JO   235

    CHAPTER THIRTY-NINE: EMI   241

    CHAPTER FORTY   247

ACKNOWLEDGMENTS   261

NOTE FROM THE AUTHOR   263

PART ONE:

EMI

CHAPTER ONE

———

Seated on the train back to Pittsburgh, Emi felt consumed with nerves. Her body buzzed from her scalp to the soles of her feet. Her family had no idea what had happened to her and assumed she was still in school, but little did they know she was four months along. At this point on her journey home, her gut looked like she had swallowed a whole loaf of sourdough bread.

She saw her mother and younger sister eagerly waiting outside of the train station. They held up a sign that boldly read, *Welcome Home Emerald*! Her artistically challenged siblings clearly produced it. Tears welled in her eyes as she knew she would disappoint them soon. Her pregnancy would never be forgiven nor forgotten by those who'd created a clear and easy path for her success. Somehow, beneath all the opportunity and care, she had still found a way to fail.

Emi quickly walked up to each of them and greeted them with a warm embrace. They had a long ride home in her mother's new Muntz Jet. Her family spoke to her rapidly, as if they planned to antagonize her since she had first left for school.

"So, darling, how is the university?" her mother asked in her uppity tone. She expected Emerald would be the same as she was, as she had participated in each club, earned perfect grades, and looked beautiful as she did.

"It's alright, Mother. It's going quite well, actually," Emi lied as she twiddled her thumbs beneath her enlarged belly. Her coat still hid her true size when she sat.

"That is lovely. As a surprise for your returning home, I planned on making pepperoni lasagna. That is still your favorite, yes?" her mother asked, and she curled her lips to reveal her dimpled cheeks. She was proud of herself and the surprise she had prepared and was eager for the special night to begin.

Emi wrapped her fingers beneath her, while her young sister was a nuisance by her side. Emi knew she would miss moments like these even though they were painfully normal. It hurt her deeply to see her family genuinely pleased to see her when she knew it would end.

In front of their home molded of scarlet brick, Emi's father stood in a freshly pressed suit and tie. He curled his lips in excitement. He stood tall with a ray of confidence. His smile glistened. When the car had rolled to its halt, Emi stepped out hesitantly. She was quickly swallowed by her father's hefty arms and hands, which reached to her small head. He squeezed her face and wrapped his meaty fingers around her hair. His cheeks glowed red, like caramel-colored apples, and his smile was wide. He looked into Emi's eyes brightly and said, "My sweet Emerald, your eyes are shining as bright as ever, and I have never been so happy to see you."

———

Months prior, as the school weeks passed, Emi waited, but she still found nothing. As she searched between her legs in the bathroom, Emi crossed her fingers and sat on the porcelain ring. She prayed to whoever would listen that a drop of blood, a spark of hope, would come out of her, but nothing ever did. As time went on, she continued to go to lectures and stroll along her college campus, as though she had not a worry in the world. The rumbling inside of her grew as a being formed inside her. There was no escape, no matter how desperately she wanted one.

Emi came from a family where failure was not an option, and education was key to success. Her family was Black and absolutely brilliant, and even though their skin ranged various shades of browns and golds, her mother swore that the Grandeur family had never been enslaved. In the year 1900, Emi's grandfather became the first Black physician in all of Pennsylvania. He had set the family up with a standard of living that had seemed impossible. Emi came from strong beliefs that God would forever lead the way, and anything less than great was a sin. Now, she had committed the worst sin of all.

It started when she met Lonnie in a poetry writing class, and she was taken by his ability to fill up a room with his undeniable charm. At the time, he'd presented himself as sweet and sophisticated. He was the type of man she imagined her family would approve of and would lead her to a happy life. But after the seed he planted inside of Emi took hold, that vision faded. It was blurred and pushed aside to make space for a new life that would come too soon.

Seated beside him one evening, in his tattered car with well-worn seats, and with the smell of his harsh cologne, Emi felt calm. She listened to the raindrops that would pitter-patter against the windshield. She felt the warmth of Lonnie's armrest in the crook of her neck, and it grew hot.

As she looked at Lonnie with eyes that had grown two sizes, uncertainty tensed every muscle. She said, "I have to tell you something." Her voice was fragile, as though she had lost it, and it grew thin with terror.

"Alright," he said suspiciously. "What is it?"

With a long lull of silence, Lonnie looked at Emi, but she was unwilling to do the same. She gazed toward the window, then stared at the rain droplets that slithered down the side of the slicked glass and melted together. "I'm late," she said and continued to look out of the window. "I think I'm pregnant."

"Well, that's alright," Lonnie said calmly, then grabbed Emi's arms gently and nudged her body toward him. She was stunned he was calmer than her. "You can have the baby, and we can start a family, Em. Is that something you would want?" he asked, his lips pressed firmly together in a tense state. He knew there were few options, to begin with, but he was still nervous about her answer.

"I would love to start a family with you," she whispered, then grabbed Lonnie's cheeks within her palms. Both of them smiled. She laughed now at how silly and nervous she had been, and she felt relieved it went so smoothly. Emi sprawled over her seat to snuggle closer to Lonnie, with his arms wrapped around her. They lay in a jubilant silence, and they squeezed one another until Emi's fear drifted with the chilled breeze.

"But you know one thing…" Lonnie said calmly but with purpose.

"What's that?" Emi smiled and exhaled, and her grip grew tighter.

"You are going to have to leave school… You know, to take care of the baby and all."

As Lonnie muttered this statement matter-of-factly, Emi loosened her grip upon him slightly. She felt the worry slip back inside of her. Her muscles tensed, and her grip, which had loosened, tightened and greased up like curly fries. "I know."

———

Emi sat at the dining table surrounded by her three sisters, mother, father, and grandparents. She knew she had to tell the truth, and there was no better time than the present. As she gazed at her family, they stuffed their faces with pieces of pepperoni coated in ricotta. They seemed to be in the best moods of their lives. Not only were they proud Emi was studying to become a nurse, but she had started college at seventeen.

"Can I tell you all something?" she finally said, despite trying to seal her lips.

Her family quickly turned toward her, and the youngest, who looked concerned about the last bite on her plate, made eye contact with Emi, then placed the cheesy morsel on her tongue.

"Now, you are all not going to be pleased with me, this was a true accident, and I believe everything will be fine." Her mother seemed terrified yet remained composed. The fear within her was hidden in the depths of her eyes as if she knew.

"You're not pregnant or something, are you? I know about your dreamboat boyfriend," her sister said jokingly. As Emi looked up, tears formed in her eyes. Her sister's cheeky smile quickly turned into a mask of utter regret, and all the color rushed out of her pudgy cheeks.

Brutal silence filled the room. Emi never heard a tone such as this. It was as if you could hear a crumb fall on the floor, and everyone would jump because the sound had been so unbelievably loud. Emi looked over at her father, and her emotions gushed out uncontrollably. His large brown eyes displayed a deep sadness. He looked as though he did not know who she was. All of them looked at her this way, and they were right. Emi was nothing more than a stranger to them now.

As Emi locked eyes with her father for a few moments longer, he opened his jaw as wide as he could manage and shouted at the top of his lungs, "I want you out of this house!"

Tears streamed down her mother's face. Her sisters reached over to their father desperately, then grabbed his arms and flopped around the dining table like fish ripped out of water.

"Daddy, no!" the youngest squealed, then reached for his grasp, but his flailing arms swiped her away. "Please don't make her leave! Let her stay, please!"

With no mind to anyone around him, he strode angrily toward Emi. Then, he grabbed her by the arm tightly and yanked her out of her seat. He walked toward the grand entrance, which now might as well have had a sign that read *No Disappointments Allowed.*

Emi quickly picked up her bag in the nick of time, and her father threw her forcefully out of the door and onto the cracked walkway. A rock scratched all the way down her cheek, and her flesh burned in the open air. Emi did not see her father close the door or what he looked like when he did, but she had a sense that she knew. He was either uncontrollably angry, with red cheeks and deep wrinkles that created canyons of rage, or his eyes were an ocean of regret. He could not turn back from his decision to disown his daughter. Although he wanted to take it back, he had considered the what-ifs, and he had to commit. Blood dripped down her cheeks and stained her glossy skin, and she held her face down. All she knew was this was the last time she would see her father in this way. This was the last time he would look at her with love in his eyes and think she was nothing less than an angel. And she was right.

CHAPTER TWO

——

After months of no longer speaking to her family, Emi's only hope out of this desperate and helpless situation was to speak to Adeline. They had met in college and related to one another from the start. Although Emi hadn't spoken to her since her departure from school, and their lives were split into diverging paths, she knew Adeline would help. Home alone, with the phone pressed to her ear, Emi listened to her phone's obnoxious ring. On the third chime, Adeline responded with her raspy voice, which made Emi break into hysteria.

"Emi? What's wrong?" Adeline asked, panicked. Her voice shook, which differed from her usual calm.

"You have to help me," Emi whimpered. She attempted to inhale all her sadness, but her emotions were evident in her shaking speech. "I have a baby now, and I don't know where to go."

As Emi's cries grew louder, Adeline listened closely. She attempted to absorb every word to understand. She wanted to know just how Emi had gotten here.

"What about Lonnie? He's with you, isn't he? And when the hell did you get pregnant?" Adeline asked, confused.

"Yes, I'm with him, but that's the problem." Emi released another cry and felt a tingling sensation grab hold of her throat. "He's getting worse, Adi. He's gambling at the clubs and not helping me at all. When he does come home, he either hits me, or he brings another woman and rubs her in my face."

The longer Emi continued, the more distraught Adeline became.

"I just need you to help me get out of here before things get too bad." Emi consciously inhaled for the first time since their conversation began. Relief filled her like a rising fog. She had not felt this light since the initial relief of Lonnie's acceptance of her pregnancy. With the return of the stress, a weight cemented itself upon her chest. She knew this would not dissipate until she made a serious change.

"Okay, Em, you just stay put, and I'll come and get the two of you right away. I promise. Just tell me where you are."

Emi breathed a sigh of relief, and after a brief conversation, hung up the phone with an abrupt clank.

As she picked up her daughter off the dusty apartment floor, she placed her on the dip of her thin waist. Then, she looked around the scattered room for her and Jo's belongings and began to pack. She felt her heartbeat within her bones, and her hands shook in fearful anticipation. Calling upon her faith, Emi hoped Adeline would arrive before Lonnie. She hoped even though her life had now been consumed by familial sin, God would listen.

———

When Emi gave birth, sweaty beads across her body plastered themselves to the thick cotton sheets. She spread her legs wide apart, in horrific pain and agony. Emi pushed out the burden that was locked inside of her for nine long months. She looked down at her wrinkled baby girl, and all she could see were round amber eyes. They resembled Emi's father's, and they contained specks of green at its center, which resembled hers. The child's skin was as smooth as silk, and she had a grin that could melt anyone's heart. Emi loved her. This creation was not a mistake, a burden, or a ruiner of lives. This was *her* Jo, and now nothing could break them apart.

Emi and Lonnie's relationship had been filled with turmoil since Emi's family said she could not see them. When she moved in with him in his shoebox apartment, with its humid, recycled air and flies that buzzed and landed on each rusty windowsill, he was in school and worked at a factory part-time. Emi was grateful for him. He provided for the baby and treated her well when he was home, but further into the pregnancy, things changed. When Emi became a bit harder to handle, and desires of food preferences and affection grew more urgent, he frolicked off with every woman in town behind her back. He believed she would never find out, and if she did, she would not mind because he had taken care of her. He was all she had.

"I just don't understand," Emi said plainly one night. Lonnie's toughened skin was caked in grease. He was still panting from his journey home. Then, he sat down to eat dinner in front of the television and did not look at her.

Emi's hands wrapped neatly around her belly, and both depression and rage consumed her face. "Lonnie, are you going to answer me? What happened to you always being there for me?" she asked in a stern voice. She held the entirety of her body still, except for a single pointer finger scraping the paint that peeled off the kitchen counter.

"I don't know what you want me to say. I think we both know why. Now you're too fat and needy. And frankly, you are becoming a pain in my hardworkin' ass. I am killing myself for the two of you, and you can't even be grateful." He turned away from the black and white screen and stared at her, with the blame-shifting.

"Listen," he said more calmly. He rose from his sunken seat and walked over to Emi, who stood in the kitchen. He grabbed her hands away from her stomach and placed them within his own. She felt the tingle of day-old grease transferred from his palms to the crevices of hers. "I know you are cooped up here all day and had to leave school, but let's face it, you were going to be a housewife pumping out kids anyway. You didn't really sacrifice a whole lot, so can you just cut me some slack, please? I'm doin' what I can."

As Emi looked up at his face, she saw confidence exude from his charming smile lines. Her stomach turned in disbelief, and she gently pulled her hands away. She tried to think of a time when she had been this upset and could not recall one. Even when her father threw her out of their home and left her with nothing more than her stuffed suitcase and bloodstained skin, it had not seemed as bad.

"I was going to be a nurse," Emi said softly, taking Lonnie aback by her remark when he had assumed the conversation was final. "I was going to finish school and be a nurse. I never wanted to be a housewife. Not like this."

He was unsure of what to say, and Emi's eyes grew a brighter shade of green from the crimson veins surrounding them. "Well," he said and turned away. "You are one now, so if I were you, I would put a stop to all of your complaining."

The longer Emi and Lonnie continued to live together, the more disappointed she became. Emi routinely waited for him to come home every night, but he only granted her wish one or two times a week. When it was, Lonnie either glued his eyes to *Gunsmoke* episodes or ate dinner and went to bed alone. The cheating, lying, and gambling became unbearable. Emi did not know if she could be with him much longer. Their relationship felt like an act of dire necessity instead of what Emi once believed was genuine love. Although Emi was pregnant before they considered marriage, she knew raising a child while unwed would cause her family to disregard her. She would be the one Grandeur family member who lost their way. She felt she was now a perpetual sinner, until death would they part.

As she looked into his grinning eyes on their wedding day, Emi felt confident marriage was the right decision, even though it was the only one. Although it was not the wedding she dreamed of as a child, and her family would not attend, she knew it was what she had to do. Although their relationship might not have been perfect and had only worsened the longer she stayed, at this moment, it had to be enough.

As she lay on their couch, which was lined in stiff plastic, she shivered. Air from the fan blew in Emi's face, and her infant wept relentlessly in her arms. She had never felt more alone. Although she was still married, Emi was no longer a wife. She was solely a mother and knew although her husband worked, with his gambling problem, he would lose far more than what he had earned. The money would grow scarcer with each passing day.

Emi pleaded with Lonnie one dawn before he left for the factory. "Lonnie, at this point, I think your problem is beyond fixing. Although I want you to stop gambling, this would go away if I found work. Just once or twice a week. That would be all."

"Emerald, you are not getting a job, and that's the end of it."
Lonnie stuffed a piece of stale bread into his chapped mouth.

"Why not?" Emi barked, and she cupped her little girl Jo tightly with her right arm. As Emi raised her voice, Jo began to yelp and shake. Small cries spurted out of her tiny frame.

"If you get a job, what does that make *me*?" Lonnie questioned, then looked at Emi fiercely. He ignored Jo's whimpers. "You will not become the man of this house, and that's final." Reaching past Emi for his keys, he marched out of the door and slammed it behind him with a bang.

Once he left the apartment, the creaking fan continued to blow, and the smell of mold seeped into the carpeted floor. She sat down and placed Jo upon her knees, then bumped them up and down to mimic being on a horse and galloping through a lively field. Emi wanted her daughter to feel like she was anywhere but here.

"You know what we are going to do, Joey?" Emi asked her daughter with a slight smirk as she continued to rise up and down. "We are going to get you out of here."

————

Emi quickly stuffed all of her and Jo's belongings into a thin garbage bag, as she anticipated her husband would come home at any minute. Then, Emi heard the phone ring, and she worried it would be Lonnie. She was relieved to hear a different voice.

"Emi, are you almost ready to go?" Adeline asked. She was in a restaurant just around the corner.

"Yes, I am. You can come on down now, and I will buzz you in, but hurry." Emi sounded panicked as the seconds ticked on.

As Adeline knocked on the door, Emi opened it, and her hands shook. Adeline placed her gaze upon Jo and became giddy.

"She's gorgeous!" she said, then hugged Emi for a moment before she picked Jo up with care.

This little girl in between Adeline's arms had never looked more beautiful or more innocent. Emi paused, and for the first time since her daughter was born, she looked at her with focus and admiration.

Then the front doorknob began to turn, and a thin pale woman tumbled inside with Emi's husband's hand in hers. Both of their bodies looked as if they had been poisoned by countless drinks, and their lungs full of cigar smoke. They had just come out of their haze from the night prior and returned to reality in the deep afternoon.

"Adeline?" Lonnie said, and he curled his face, feeling conflicted. "What are you doing here?" As he ripped his hand away from the intoxicated woman, he moved closer to Emi. Adeline held Jo tightly and took a few steps back.

"Lonnie, we are leaving. Emi can't stay here anymore."

"You can't leave! You're mine!" he barked and attempted to rip Jo away from Adeline's arms.

Adeline turned her back, and Emi stepped in front of them as an act of defense.

"Lonnie, I can't stay." Emi's voice shook, and she planted her feet into the floor to block Jo and Adeline from him. "You are just getting worse. Jo I can't live like this."

Lonnie slapped Emi with a stinging clap. She fell on the floor and winced from the pain. Adeline pushed Lonnie away and protected Emi.

"We are leaving, and there's nothing you can do about it!" Adeline yelped. She helped Emi up and propped Jo's pudgy legs in place with one arm. "And if it isn't clear pal, she's filing for divorce."

Emi stood and looked at this man she had once loved with disappointment. She felt her cheek throb as it began to bruise. She grabbed Adeline's nimble hand and squeezed it tight, then walked away.

CHAPTER THREE

———

As Emi resided within Adeline's home for a few months, she began to feel more composed. Although Adeline was at work for most of the day, Emi found comfort in her time home with Jo. As their bond grew, it felt like this child she once labeled as a mistake became her greatest miracle. Jo sprouted daily. At times, it even felt she had growth spurts hour by hour. At a time when Emi felt like everyone tried to escape her presence, Jo seemed like all she had. Out of everyone Emi had met, Jo was the best by a long shot.

When Emi moved into Adeline's apartment, it felt like she traveled back in time and was in college again. As she walked through the nicked doorway, Jo's dainty chestnut arms reached up and tugged the bouncing wisps of her mother's tightly pinned hair. Emi knew this new place would accept them both, and Adeline would help more than her family or an estranged Lonnie ever could.

Emi returned to her college campus as a guest in another woman's crowded home. Meanwhile, she found this was the best place she could think of to keep away from the man who had caused her so much grief. Although Lonnie knew Adeline, he did not know where she lived, and with so many homes scattered across campus, they would be impossible to find.

Adeline was known as the life of the party and captured the affection of every boy in her company. When she went out at night and woke with the stench of beer on her tongue and a throbbing headache, she wanted Emi to join her on these youthful adventures. However, every time Adeline brought it up, Emi managed to talk herself out of it.

"Come on, Emi! You're eighteen now! I can't even believe you started college so young, and now you have no time to waste. You must go to a party with me immediately, and you can meet my boyfriend's new friend! He's such a fox and seems a lot better than the loser who knocked you up." Adeline sat politely on the tired sofa beside Emi. As she rocked her arms back and forth in a playful manner, Adeline attempted to pull a reaction out of her. She managed to break Emi's stern face into a cheeky grin.

"Adi, you know I can't," Emi said. "I have Jo, and no one will be able to watch her. Not to mention I don't want to be roaming around campus. What if Lonnie finds me?"

Emi's eyes grew more concerned, and Jo flailed about in her lap between thin legs dressed in snagged nylon stockings. Adeline shifted her gaze from Emi to Jo and began to smile. Then she leaned toward her as light danced in her eyes.

"Okay, okay." Adeline rubbed Jo's small hands and rocked them back and forth. She ceased Jo's fussing and morphed her uncomfortable sounds into joyous giggles. "Don't go, but one of these days, Emi. I will ask around and see if anyone is up to take care of Jo for a night so you can live every once in a while."

"Alright, alright," Emi huffed. "Have fun tonight."

"Oh, I will," Adeline said playfully. She smiled widely and skipped back to her bathroom to doll herself up for the evening ahead.

———

Emi awoke later than usual one morning, still in her worn, blush-colored robe. She lifted Jo from her slumber and tucked her within the crease of her right arm. They headed for the kitchen. Emi's naked toes pressed against the chipped tile floor as she prepared scrambled eggs for the three of them with her free hand. She scraped her spatula across the hot skillet as the eggs puffed up from the mixture of whole milk within them. She had learned this trick for her mother. It was what her entire family claimed as the secret to the Grandeurs' *perfect pillow eggs.*

Emi knocked lightly on Adeline's door frame and held out a plate of pillowy eggs and white toast while Jo hung from her side. After a few moments, and with no response, Emi slid into the room and completed her usual routine. She woke Adeline up on the weekends and shook her from her alcohol-induced coma. Adeline cracked her eyes open and revealed remnants of mascara chunks glued to her lashes. Eyeliner seeped from her lid down to her foundation-splotched cheeks. Adeline grunted and cleared her throat. Emi heard a light knock on the front door.

Emi made her way to answer it as Adeline remained in the comfort of her bed. She had only begun to wake from the dark smell of newly ground coffee. Emi placed her ear against the closed entrance to listen for a voice. She searched for any sound to break through the thumping undertone of her accelerated heart to confirm it was not Lonnie. After listening for a while and hearing only muttered conversation in low tones, she decided it was not Lonnie. Lonnie's voice mimicked a chime and was soothing yet sharp.

"Is Adeline even here? No one's answering," a voice said faintly through the paneled wood, impatient.

"Yes, she's here. Just wait, she's probably still asleep." another responded, then knocked on the door again and startled Emi and Jo alike. The light taps now turned into the banging of a sledgehammer.

As Emi opened the door slowly, two husky men stood before her. They were well over six feet tall and had complexions that mimicked a batch of rich chocolate fudge. After they all linked eyes, Emi's mouth nearly hit the floor. She looked at them for longer than normal and said nothing. Then she tilted her neck down a few inches to find the two men sported letterman jackets that read on the front patch, *University of Pennsylvania Football Team 1953.*

As Emi was unsure of what to say but felt uncomfortable with the silence, Adeline walked out of her room. She skipped with desire as if she was a child headed for a delicious treat.

"Hi!" she said and jumped into one of the burly men's arms. His thick jacket sleeves wrapped tightly around her, and after their release, they exchanged a soft peck.

"Emi, I've told you about my boyfriend, Dale, right?" Adeline said, and her cheeks flushed.

"Yes, I've definitely heard a lot about him," Emi said more comfortably, now that Adeline's bright presence had broken the tension. "How are you?"

"I'm doing well," he said in a smooth voice. "Your name is Emerald, right?"

"Yes, but I usually go by Emi." As Emi and Dale smiled at one another, she sunk into the situation as if it was a new plush mattress and looked at Adeline, who gave her an animated expression.

"Also, Emi, this is Dale's best buddy and the *very* eligible bachelor and football star, Sonny Sanders."

When Emi turned to look at Sonny, who stood there silently for the entirety of the group's encounter, she was baffled by how far she had cocked her head to meet him. His broad shoulders and athletic build intimidated her, but when she finally reached his soft eyes, he cracked the widest smile she had ever seen. Emi melted.

"How are ya?" he said, and he made heavy eye contact with her. When he began to lean down and in, Emi did not know if it was for a hug or a kiss on the cheek, but to her bewilderment, he reached across to take hold of Jo. His expression searched for consent, and as Emi nodded awkwardly, he grabbed Jo. The child's hands intertwined within Emi's half-tamed hair. Sonny helped to coil each strand out from her stubby fingers.

"You have such a beautiful daughter," he said, with Jo propped in his secure arms and raised a foot higher. "You know, she looks just like you, but with a little more color on her."

Emi held his gaze, and a burning sensation grew in her throat. Once she realized this, she looked at Dale and Adeline once again for a distraction. She wanted to keep her emotions from boiling over.

When Adeline, Dale, and Emi all sat on the cramped old couch, they were captivated by how Sonny behaved with Jo. The two of them sat down on the carpeted floor, and as Sonny supported Jo before him, a bright smile beamed on Jo's face.

"Okay, I don't know about you, but Sonny's whole dad act is turning me on," Adeline whispered to Emi, and they both giggled discreetly.

"Your boyfriend is *right here*," Emi said, and the two of them laughed even harder than before. Both men looked at each other quizzically.

As Emi inspected this man she had just met, who took up the entirety of Adeline's living room floor and held Jo with such careful intention, she had never known so confidently someone would make a good parent. As Emi sat and watched the love Sonny seemed to have for a child he just met that morning, she admired him. She was unsure if she would love someone else's child so quickly.

That day, whenever Emi looked at Sonny for a moment, he always caught her gaze and grinned. Even when she thought she looked away discreetly, it was never a success, and the more times she was caught, the louder Sonny chuckled. Emi only became more confused as to why she did it anyway. She did not know what she was thinking and believed nothing would ever come of this. But although Emi was still a married woman on the run, a small gleam of hope billowed deep inside of her for the possibility she might become friends with Sonny and more possibly.

CHAPTER FOUR

———

As the weeks rushed by, Jo grew faster than Emi had imagined possible. Adeline and Sonny became Emi's biggest support systems and greatest friends. When Adeline attended a class or worked in the early mornings, Sonny always stopped by and stayed awhile. He helped Emi take care of Jo and let her breathe and walk away when the stress had become too overwhelming to handle alone. Sonny played with Jo often and quickly obtained the ability to stop her tears with the snap of a finger.

Once a week, Emi called Sonny for help when she searched for work. She was open-minded, but no one gave her the time of day. Although Emi was extremely bright and told her possible managers about her education and family background, it seemed as though, whenever she showed her face in the establishment, her fair caramel skin turned all her hard work into a waste of time.

"Hello. My name is Emerald Grandeur," she said calmly one afternoon. She'd left the apartment just thirty minutes prior and made her way to one of the more popular restaurants in the area. It was always packed with students and businessmen, and Emi heard they had the best burgers and fries in the city. As she introduced herself to one of the employees, everyone looked at her. She was dressed in her nicest dress with freshly applied makeup, which brought out the shining of her speckled eyes. They would dismiss her before she had even been given a chance.

"I'm sorry, girl," one of the restaurant managers began, and he towered over Emi's slight body behind the counter. He looked like he was toughened up by the grease and hard work he had just escaped from. "This here job is not for a colored girl. I misunderstood on the phone. I believed you were white."

Her face no longer wore an expression of disappointment or surprise at these times, only a saddened understanding. "Alright, well, thank you kindly, sir," she responded politely. As she walked out of the door, a few of the customers stared at her. Others were unwilling to even spare a glance, and embarrassment burned Emi's face to a shining red.

The more Sonny came over, as Emi continued to look for work, the more she missed him when he was gone. Both Emi and Jo missed Sonny's presence and his ability to bring forth an indescribable sense of comfort. Although Emi and Jo both felt his bitter absence, the more she took time away from him, the more selfish and responsible she felt. She was taking precious college moments away from him. She would see him play with Jo or prepare meals for her when she looked for work or took a nap, and she felt guilty. She was the one who had gotten pregnant in school, and it was her responsibility to take care of the baby, not his. His role was to be a student, a football player, and to have fun and make mistakes while he still could.

Sonny tapped lightly on the door with his large and steady knuckles, and as he stepped through, he and Emi looked at one another. She knew today would be the day when they would talk. She wanted to discuss how he had become more of a resident rather than a friend who provided a helping hand every now and again.

As Emi sat beside him on the hideously floral printed couch, she rested. Then, Jo squished between Sonny's muscular legs, and she looked happy as ever. Sonny looked happier than Emi had wanted him to.

"I think that we need to talk," Emi said softly, then turned toward them.

"What about?" he replied, with a smile, then chuckled as Jo swayed back and forth on his legs.

"You know I'm grateful to you for coming over to take care of Jo. It really means a lot to me. But I just feel like we are getting in the way of you enjoying your freedom. Jo is not yours, and I feel like maybe I have done something to where you believe you need to take care of her. I would never want to put that burden on you."

Lifting Jo up from under her armpits, Sonny placed her between himself and Emi. Then, he reached over and grabbed Emi's hands tenderly. The feeling of his tough hands dug into her smooth fingertips and relaxed her.

"Emi, I love being here with you and Jo. I know it's college, and people are supposed to party and do stupid things, but I'm enjoying myself more than ever."

Sonny looked at Emi intensely, and she nodded.

"Are you sure? If you change your mind and don't want to come by one day, then I completely understand." She could not stop her guilty conscience.

"Emi, just stop," he replied, then squeezed her hand tighter. "I love spending time with the both of you. I mean that."

He began to lean in slowly, then moved his hands and reached up to her unmade face. The warmth from her skin ran into his palms and through his veins. Emi looked at him, unsure if she should lean in as well or reject the idea in its entirety. Sonny began to reach over Jo to Emi, and the tension grew between them. When their lips were a breath away, the front door flew open, and Sonny returned to his original position. This also caused him to pull Jo toward him, which made it seem as though he'd held her in his lap all this time. They turned their heads and saw who had marched through. Adeline stood proudly in the center of the doorway and looked over to see Sonny and Emi closer than they had ever been before. Emi's hand still rested upon Sonny's leg, and once she noticed, she quickly withdrew it into her own lap. When Emi grew flushed and Sonny awkward, Adeline smiled.

———

The next night was Adeline's birthday, which she had looked forward to for weeks. She planned to drown her academic sorrows in tequila shots and go out to the local-colored bars with Dale, but she felt bad Emi could not come. Emi still did not feel comfortable spending a night away from Jo but asked Sonny if he would stay with her, even though she had just said they spend too much time together. It was not that Emi wanted Sonny to herself or felt jealous of his adventures, but when he was gone, it felt as though her body went hollow, and all the fear of Lonnie and abandonment of her family crept into her mind.

As they leaned back on the couch, with Jo between them and two healthy servings of mac and cheese on the coffee table, Sonny and Emi found themselves comfortable. Emi was now able to crack jokes and reveal her authentic personality, which she had only shown to her sisters and Adeline.

As *I Love Lucy* came to an end, the television switched to *Gunsmoke*, which Emi despised. She had not realized how close in proximity the two of them had gotten. They nearly squished the life out of Jo, who leaned back on the pit of the sofa constrained by each of their legs. Emi pulled herself away and placed Jo in the center of her lap. She could tell from the look in Jo's eyes, which was like frosted glass, it was time for her to lie down and dream into tomorrow.

When she returned to her seat after putting Jo to bed, Sonny was more awake than he had been in the past half-hour. He scanned Emi as she approached him. His eyes sparked with newfound energy as he looked at her with care.

"Emi, can I talk to you about something?" he asked shyly, unable to take his eyes away from her. His voice sounded incredibly thin.

As Emi sat down, he reached for her hands, but this touch felt different than before. She felt his calloused skin as he stroked his fingers on the back of her hands. His fingertips hovered over her freckled flesh and ran them along her purple veins.

"I've meant to say this for a while, but I've been too scared to speak up," he said. He watched his fingers rub back and forth against her hand.

Emi perked up and paid close attention. She thought she knew what he would say but could not be sure. His chin pointed slightly downward as if he was ashamed. Emi knew she had never seen him look more nervous. His frame and body language resembled the *Statue of David*. Sonny looked beautiful.

"Sure, what is it, Sonny?" she questioned. She did not want to break the silence.

As he opened his lips, a sound almost squeaked out of them, and the sentence he had wanted to tell Emi degraded into inaudible words. There was a slight knock on the door, and after remaining unanswered for a few moments, it became a thundering bang.

"Hey, open up!" a raging voice howled. Emi recognized the high-pitched rasp and anger in his inflections. The thought of what would happen sent a running shiver through each limb and her body quivered in horror.

Quickly perking up, Sonny walked to the door. Sonny looked at Emi's fright with confusion. As he leaned against the thinned pine frame, he knew he would have to open it sometime but could not lift a finger.

"Who is it?" he asked through the wall. Emi wanted to answer but only produced mutters. Sonny reached for the knob and opened the door slowly. Emi quickly jumped to hide behind the great mass of his body. Every muscle grew tense as she waited.

"There you are," he smirked, then walked through the door and over to Emi.

"Wait," Sonny said quickly, then moved his arm up to block the man. "Who are you, and what are you doing here?" he asked, unaware of what happened. He tried to seem brave for Emi's sake.

"She didn't tell you?" the stranger questioned and began to laugh hysterically. His high-pitched cackles filled the nipping evening wind and flowed through the open door. Meanwhile, Sonny looked unamused.

"I'm her *husband.*"

CHAPTER FIVE

―――

Emi stood behind Sonny and looked at the man on the other side of the door. She'd once loved him so dearly but now felt debilitating fear.

Sonny turned to her, entirely befuddled. "Is that true? You're *married*?"

Emi was unable to pluck the perfect words from her chaotic scramble of thought to explain. She only nodded her head to confirm. Lonnie began to laugh dramatically and leaned on the door. His high-pitched shriek rose in volume, and Sonny became angry.

"Well, this is just great," Lonnie said as he continued his arrogant huffs. "What? Did you really think while she was off hiding away, y'all were *family*?" His laughter grew, and he grasped his knees in amusement. "That is *so sweet*."

While Emi felt fearful, Sonny looked bitter. His near heartbreak quickly shifted to a mode of protection. He leaned his arm back behind him and held Emi's side to make sure she was all right.

"You need to get outta here," Sonny said confidently. "If she's hiding out here, she clearly doesn't want to see you."

Lonnie tried to settle down, but after a few chuckles, he bit Sonny with a response. "Fine, fine. I'll go. But Emi," he said, then cocked his head around Sonny's broad shoulder to peer into her fearful eyes. She looked at him and thought of Jo. She hoped she would not make a sound from the other room. "When you're done playing house with this overgrown gorilla, then you'll know where to find—"

Before he finished, Sonny's fist tightened in one motion and slammed into the side of Lonnie's cheek. He knocked him to the hard floor, and his tense laugh pierced their ears again. Emi had once found that annoying laugh endearing, but now, it made her stomach twist with bile-infested disgust.

"Don't worry, old boy. I'm leaving," Lonnie said, then stood up slowly and held his thin arms up in surrender. "You can have her. She's eighteen and already washed up, but just so I make the message loud and clear: Jo will *never* be yours, no matter how often you come over to play daddy. Even if I never see that kid again, she's *my blood*. Every time you tuck her in and read her a bedtime story, you remember this moment, and you remember *me*."

Lonnie walked off, down the staircase, and into the foggy darkness of the Pennsylvania night. Sonny slowly closed the door. He only broke his eyes away as the click of the door brought him back to their harsh reality.

"Are you alright?" Sonny asked calmly, then turned to face Emi and placed each of his sweaty palms on her cheeks.

"I am so sorry, Sonny." Emi sighed as tears welled in her eyes, and her hands shook. "I feel so terrible."

"It's alright, really," he said, and Emi only became more frustrated with herself.

"No, it's not! I didn't even tell you I was *married*. I like you, and I shouldn't have hidden something like this," she confessed. Sonny looked at her, concerned, and then plainly. His puffy cheeks fell flat, and the creases along his forehead evaporated.

"I like you too."

Sitting back down on the sofa, Sonny exhaled loudly, and sweat ran down his temples and alongside his sharp cheekbones. Emi brought Jo back out and held her tightly. She was afraid of Lonnie's return and felt the need to bring her out of her isolation into their company. They played with the baby to keep her from crying and turned a program on the television. Both Sonny and Emi's hearts beat rapidly, and Emi sat back in disbelief. Sonny looked over to Emi slowly. His eyes were wide as if he had seen a ghost, and his once rich complexion grew gray as the night continued.

"Emi, I hope you know, I'm not trying to take the place of Jo's father. I would never try to do that. I just–"

"Stop." Emi interrupted and then smiled. "You are more of a father to Jo than Lonnie ever was. That is why we are getting a divorce."

"What made him a bad father?" Sonny asked timidly.

"He's a liar, cheater, and gambler, and he couldn't give less of a shit about Jo or me. I'm glad he's out of our life, and I would rather die than go back to that son of a bitch."

With the beginnings of a smile, Sonny reached over and cupped Jo under her stout arm, then placed her in between each of their legs as usual. He leaned her against the couch and reached across her tiny body once again, but this time, he came closer to Emi's lips. Sonny's mouth stuck to Emi's, and his hand reached to cup her face with care. He shifted his hand to the back of her neck and twirled his pointer finger within her tawny-colored hair. When their soft lips met and parted, Sonny looked into Emi's blazing eyes and took a deep breath.

"Marry me."

This proposition was unexpected but sincere. Emi looked into his deep eyes and lips, now stained in the center from her rose lipstick, and she kissed him again. She held his palm in place on her warmed cheek, and the two of them released simultaneously for a tight embrace. Emi was elated, and Sonny had never felt more grateful.

CHAPTER SIX

—

Sonny and Emi were at the end of a process more tedious than either of them imagined. Emi had handled the divorce, and Lonnie relinquished custody. Emi felt a sense of relief the whole process haunting her thoughts consistently had ended. Through all the bickering and Lonnie's journey to find Emi, it had reached a point where he no longer cared.

Freshly out of a marriage and with a desire for a new beginning, Emi's love for Sonny grew stronger as time passed. But she did not want to jump into something.

"Do you think we are getting into this a little too fast?" Emi asked Sonny one evening. Stuffed in Adeline's narrow kitchen, they were preparing their new favorite meal of Sloppy Joes and a juicy half-watermelon each. The two of them dug dull silver spoons into their rind bowls for full sweet bites and spat the seeds into a ceramic dish.

"I agree you are switching husbands pretty quickly," he joked, and Emi hit him playfully across the arm. "But I love you, Emi. And if you think about it, I've known you for quite some time now, enough time to be sure I want you to be my wife."

Although doubt poked through the shadows of Emi's subconscious, Sonny reassured her in the way his eyes glinted in her presence. He constantly showed up for her and Jo without fail.

"This is what I want, Sonny," she told him. "You are everything I've ever wanted. I just didn't know it would happen so soon, and so easily, and to be honest, it seems a bit surreal."

———

Emi cultivated a newly found freedom with a loving man by her side. After the divorce was finalized, the air had been clearer, along with the worries and what-ifs. She felt only confidence regarding her future.

"You know, I've been thinking," Sonny quietly said, sprawled on Adeline's couch with Jo laying on top of his firm stomach.

Looking over at him, Emi had many ideas of what he was going to say. *You should go back to school. You should move out of Adeline's apartment and in with me.* But as he looked at her, he reached for both her hand and Jo's. "What do you think of me adopting Jo? And becoming her father."

Emi had expected, at some point, Sonny would take the full-time role of Jo's father, but she had never considered adoption.

"You still have a year of school left. Are you sure you want to do that?" Emi asked, concerned he did not know what he was getting himself into.

"You know, when I was young, my mother left me, and I didn't have a father," Sonny said quietly, then curled into himself.

"What do you mean?" Emi could not fathom being a child without anyone to call mother or father.

"My mother had me out of wedlock," he began, then rubbed his palms together stiffly in his lap. He looked away. "She didn't know who my father was, and she always bounced around from boyfriend to boyfriend. They always hit her, or me, or they left us when they decided being a family would be too much. When she had enough and wanted to start a new life, she ran away with her new love interest of the month and sent me to Oklahoma to live with my aunt. I always just wished my mother would come back, or I would find out who my father was, but I never did. I haven't seen her since the day she dropped me off and left me. That was ten years ago."

Emi did not know what to say but instead grabbed Sonny's hands and rubbed them tenderly. She looked at his dimmed light and pecked him on the cheek.

He smiled. "I just want to be a great father to Jo."

"You will be," Emi responded, then leaned her head in the pit of his neck. She rested her full weight on his shoulder and side. Sonny released his hand from her interlocked fingers and grazed them across the small of her back.

As Sonny broke away from Emi and began to hold Jo's two hands with his right one, Emi saw the way her daughter looked up at him. She beamed with warmth whenever she saw Sonny. This was something Emi had not entirely appreciated until now. Although she knew they were close, Emi was able to see how much he cared for Jo and how Jo cared for him.

"Do you think Jo will ever ask about Lonnie? If she will want to find him or talk to him when she's older?" Sonny asked Emi as he switched his gaze from Jo's bubbling smile to her.

"Why would she want to do that when she has a father as great as you? Lonnie only created her, but you will raise her and help her discover who she wants to be."

CHAPTER SEVEN

——

Five years later…

Emi and Sonny's life of cramped apartments, where they walked the streets of Philadelphia and feared Lonnie, faded into the distance. Once they married, they agreed to move to Washington state for Sonny's work as a psychologist after his schooling had ceased. It was time to leave Pennsylvania. It was a place riddled with memories of home she would now dismiss for an eternity.

Since the day Emi was excused from her childhood home, she never heard from her family and could not build the strength to reach out herself. Although she knew she was a disappointment to them, as a prime example to her younger sisters of who not to be, she thought of them often. She wondered how her sisters were doing and if they had grown taller and more beautiful. Judgmental explanations for her absence and foggy recollections replaced their memories of their oldest sister. She especially wondered about their father, if she would ever talk to him, see his face, or feel his warmth and affection.

The day before the move, Sonny held Jo's hand and packed with his other. As he worked, Emi decided to return home. She felt a calling to revisit a part of her life, and she wondered if, after all these years, the pleasant recollection of her had become forgotten. She wondered if he would look at her as an unwelcome stranger, and she desperately hoped he wouldn't.

"Are you sure that's a good idea?" Sonny asked reluctantly as he sat on their tired sofa and shared a large root beer float with Jo. "I just don't want you to get hurt. If your father said you're no longer a part of the family, then I don't think you showing up at their front door is going to end well."

"I need to try," Emi said and felt a tingling emptiness in her stomach. She knew, although she was nervous now, she would regret not trying. It would become too late for redemption. "I just have to."

———

As Emi rode the train home, she remembered her last trip too well. She was terrified by the answers she would receive in the next few hours and was certain, after this trip, she would know if she had a family outside of Sonny and Jo. Looking out through a large window, she watched as the autumn trees danced by. Her stomach bubbled, and her limbs went numb.

Am I ready to see them again? Am I ready to be disowned once and for all, to be an orphan, even though both of my parents are alive and well and simply don't want me? I don't think I'm ready. But if I don't go now, then I'll never be.

Emi walked out of the train station among the sea of bodies that pushed and prodded past. Meanwhile, she fought the sensation and to find a cab to escape from the chaos, and the car pulled out from the curb and onto the road. As she drew closer to her inevitable future, Emi's heart drummed faster. Her sensation of fear and excitement rolled into one with dread tightly intertwined.

As she saw her home for the first time since she had been banished, Emi stood in awe. She had forgotten how magnificent it was. Built from pristine crimson brick, with ivy branches draped along the vast walls and windowsills, it was the Grandeurs' palace. Everyone who walked by wished they lived there, and they were unable to fathom a Black family owned it proudly, and they'd earned every square foot and commanded their high status.

As Emi closed the car door gently and walked up with reticence, silence filled her ears, aside from the clicks of her kitten heels grinding against the fine stone. As she reached the main door, Emi stood still. Then, she lifted her hand slowly and produced three soft clicks with the gold door knocker. The base was a strong lion head, and Emi fondly remembered the feline face from childhood. The door swung open.

"Emerald?" her father gasped. His eyes grew large, and his mouth gaped open to reveal the lower half of his perfectly shaped teeth. "What are you doing here?"

As Emi looked at him, with his impeccable caramel skin and dark hair that had new streaks of silver, trimmed to mere waves instead of full curls, Emi began to cry. The emotion brought a tickle to her throat, and she felt frustrated with herself for revealing herself so quickly.

"I missed you, Daddy," she whimpered, then leaned in for a hug. Her father moved his body away in horror, and he crossed his arms in front of his chest.

"You need to go," he said, emotionless, though Emi saw a slight twitch in his lip. After one blink, he started to shed a tear. The saltwater slowly pushed out of its socket and painted his eyes a deeper shade of brown.

"Please just talk to me," Emi replied, her inflection full of emotion. Her father backed away and slammed the door in her face. Emi only heard his dress shoe heels as he walked through the enclosed hall and to her sister inside. Their voices sounded deeper, and to Emi, almost unrecognizable.

"Who was that?" one of the girls inside asked. When Emi leaned against the sanded wood and listened in on the conversation, she heard her father painfully clear.

"It was no one," he said bluntly. He breathed in a sharp sniffle to collect all his running mucus and shame. "No one at all."

Emi knew now she would never see her sisters' toothy, awkward smiles of adolescence and her mother's comforting meals of pepperoni lasagna. She would never see her father's delicate skin, his curly salt and pepper hair, and his rooted eyes, which used to look at her with love. The emerald specks of her own eyes were animated by her tears of mourning, and although beautiful, her father would never see them again.

———

When Emi arrived in Tacoma, Washington, it felt like being transported into another world. With Sonny's new job, his schedule full of appointments and meetings, Emi returned to the life she knew. She sat in a quaint house, now within the shade of evergreen trees, and she cooked, cleaned, and spent time with her forever-growing Jo.

Now that Jo was five years old and hurtling toward womanhood faster than Emi had believed possible, Emi sensed her slipping away. Jo became less interested in helping with everyday chores, cuddles on the couch, and reading the old fables. Jo still loved her mother, and at times, like every five-year-old, craved the moments of baking and reading stories. But she did not need her in the same way.

The more Jo ran off and played with her dolls, the more Emi thought of what she wanted to do next, who she wanted to be, other than a mother and housewife. At times, she reflected on when she was confident her destiny would lead to something more. Once, Emi wanted to be a nurse, and she still did every once in a while, as she pictured herself in the bright white uniform, as she assisted those in need. As she imagined these fictional situations and this once attainable life, she would smile to herself. All of the possibilities still remained for her, and she dreamt of a time when those wants and desires could become a reality.

After Sonny's first work week, Emi spent all week practicing how she would present these thoughts and desires to him.

"Sonny, you know I've been thinking," Emi began, once her proposition became a well-rehearsed monologue. Sonny shifted to his side. Jo laid on her back in between them, and Emi continued, "Ever since having Jo, I have been alone a lot and at home all of the time. I've been thinking about this for a long time, but I've just been too nervous to say it to you."

Sonny's thick eyebrows furled, and his eyes shrank into a squint.

"What is it?" he asked calmly, but he sounded uncertain.

"I want to work. I want to get out of the house and get a job or even go back to school and become a nurse. I just want to do something for *me*."

After she said this, her chest pumped up and down from the increase of her heart rate and erratic breath. For a while, Sonny said nothing, and Emi's head spun as she considered what circled her mind. After Sonny rested in his silence, he parted his lips and inhaled deeply.

"I don't think that's a good idea," he said softly, and his hands began to tense even before the response was finished. "You need to stay home with Jo and cook and clean and take care of our house. It wouldn't make sense for you to get a job. Not right now."

Emi swiveled her head to the television screen to distract herself, but she was overwhelmed. At that moment, Sonny was sad for Emi. He felt bad for what he had said but believed it was the right thing, not only for him and his needs but also for the family.

"Okay," Emi said with a crack of heartache, then turned away from Sonny to her opposite side and closed her eyes and awaited sleep. She listened to the television's static in the background. "I understand."

CHAPTER EIGHT

———

As Sonny became more comfortable, their choices began to revolve around his needs in lieu of Emi's. Although he felt pleased with their decision to move, he prioritized his time differently than before. He still loved Jo and Emi but was never around to see either one of them. It began a month after they arrived, and this pattern formed and ensued.

"Hey, sorry I'm late," Sonny said to Emi and kissed Jo on the side of her forehead as he sat down at the dinner table. The two of them had waited for him once again, for nearly an hour, and this same routine recurred every night. As a result, Emi had to reheat their meals each night, hoping that soon something would change.

"Sonny, you need to stop doing this," Emi responded in a whining tone. She was happy he had found a group of friends and had joined the Black slow-pitch league in their county, but now Sonny seemed to enjoy that more than eating a meal with his own family.

"I know, and I'm sorry. The team just runs a bit late sometimes," he responded, then got up once again and washed his dirty hands in the kitchen sink. He still had dirt packed under his nail beds. Sitting back down, he ate while Emi said grace to herself.

"So, how was your day?" Emi asked calmly.

"It was the same as usual."

As he stared down at his plate of ketchup-smothered meatloaf and bacon mashed potatoes, he did not lift his head or address his wife and daughter. Jo ached for her father's attention which she was now used to not receiving. She turned her head down.

As Sonny stuffed his face with the tang of tomato and cream, silence crept its way back into the room. Although Emi craved to discuss her day and Jo's first day of school, Sonny did not seem to care. It seemed as though he would rather be in their presence without saying a word because, for him, that would pass the time more quickly.

———

As Emi lay in bed, wide awake, she pretended to be asleep. Sonny slid under the duvet and attempted not to wake her, even though his stealthy silence was unnecessary. As he turned to his side and faced the bedroom window, he did not think to give his wife a touch, kiss, or any tenderness. Emi's eyes began to water, and her throat burned. She craved his attention, but it was clear he only desired sleep.

Does he not love us anymore? Emi stuffed her cries deep into her pillow. *Is he cheating on me?*

Although this was the first time she had asked herself this question, she could not contain her worry. Though Emi had once considered Sonny entirely different from Lonnie, their resemblance had become uncanny, and even comparing these two men who she'd once believed to be widely different brought Emi's anxiety to a new high.

When Emi awoke the following morning, her cheeks were slippery from the anguish of the prior night. She turned over to look at Sonny. He was gone, and the left side of the bed was awry with his tangled duvet. Sonny had not even whispered a farewell in her ear as he used to, and he had not said when he would return. *When does a husband come home after a date with his mistress?* Emi's head spun. She needed to decide for herself what to do. Although she still loved Sonny dearly and knew once he had felt the same, she had to do something for herself, which she had not done since she told her parents of her pregnancy. She needed to get away, not for her daughter and not for Sonny, but for herself.

As Emi leaned on the kitchen counter and chopped carrots for that night's dinner, Jo skipped around the living room sofa and sang along to the fuzzed radio. Meanwhile, Sonny trudged through the door and looked more tired than before. He gave Jo a quick kiss on her forehead and gave Emi a simple wave and hello.

"You're home on time for once," Emi said sourly.

Sonny quickly turned his head from Jo to finally look Emi in the eye. He was confused and offended by her sharp tone.

"What's your problem?" he asked, puzzled. Emi stared at him with strength in her voice, and she crossed her arms and furled her eyebrows. She took a deep breath and did what she promised herself she would do. *For me.*

"I'm leaving for a week," she said sternly.

Sonny looked at Emi with her arms tightly wound and her mouth molded into a stern curl. At first, he chuckled and assumed this was a joke, but she continued, "That will give you some time to be alone with your daughter, who you haven't been paying much attention to recently. Maybe when I return, you'll treat me like your *wife* instead of your housemaid."

His chuckling ceased.

CHAPTER NINE

—

As Emi drove off in their Jeep Wagoneer, she inhaled the undertones of french fries and old baby powder. She did not know where she was headed, but at this point, she did not care. All she knew was she wanted to get away from Sonny, and she hoped, upon her return, he would become the person she knew.

Ten hours was longer than Emi anticipated being on the road. Distracted by her thoughts and oblivious to the direction she was headed, she drove until her fingers ached from the gripping of the wide steering wheel, and her legs swelled from their cramped position. She cycled through different emotions throughout the drive. It was exhausting being alone. But this act of leaving her family, and leaving Jo, was temporary.

When her bodily discomfort reached an unbearable point, Emi pulled off the freeway in a small town in Montana. Soaring, thin trees concealed Choteau, and the air was crisp enough to dry her throat and leave its tinge of maple. This was a place where she had never been, and she hoped for some self-discoveries while she was away. Emi was unable to recall when she last traveled a journey by herself for sole pleasure and was confident this was the beginning of her journey to become her own person.

Emi drove into a motel parking lot. Her family had never gone to motels since her father could afford higher-class hotels. Now, she would not receive special treatment. She was just Emi Sanders. After she checked in and was assigned a room, Emi was convinced it would contain webs from thin eerie spiders and huddled families of mice. She grabbed her bag full of clothes, books, and journals and walked into the room. After she took a few steps into the cracked doorway, she noticed the carpet was stained with mysterious substances, and the reeking odor of sweat and dust wafted into the air.

"Where am I?" Emi whispered to herself, horrified. She reminded herself having a room that met her previous familial standards was not the point of this journey. Leaving Sonny was for a greater purpose. He needed to spend time with Jo to see who he would leave behind if he continued to distance himself from her. It was no longer about Emi's sexual desires or ache for attention. Now, it was about the future. When Jo reflected on her adolescence, Emi hoped she would remember Sonny as a loyal and good man.

———

After Emi wandered the town's streets for a few days, around the strip of clothing stores and restaurants, she acted as a fly on the wall to the local lives. Meanwhile, she admired the families that walked together and visited bakeries for wholesome breakfasts and roamed around bookstores. These were activities Emi desperately wanted to do with her own family but had not in years. She wanted to explore the streets of this new Washington city her family had just moved to months ago. However, she had only left her own neighborhood to pick up Jo from school and for her weekly visits to the grocery store.

Emi wanted Sonny to take her out to dinner so she did not have to cook every day. She wanted them to visit a bookstore, which he knew had been her favorite place in the entire world. The last time he had done this was the day he adopted Jo years ago. After, it seemed like, for him, the novelty of having a family dissipated as he began to focus on money, sports, and his own needs.

Why doesn't Sonny want to do these things with me? Emi asked herself multiple times while she roamed Choteau, though she could not find an answer. Emi had not wanted to be a mother so soon and had goals for herself. But ever since her pregnancy, she'd left everything to provide for Jo. This was the only way, but even with these unplanned changes, she felt a lingering hope. Perhaps, she should no longer sacrifice herself. She could become as selfish as Sonny.

For the entirety of the trip, Emi said nothing, aside from brief coffee orders. Emi's thoughts remained internal, and she contemplated questions regarding Jo and Sonny and what *she* wanted out of life. If Sonny could not free up his time for his own family, let her pursue bigger dreams, or give her a simple kiss goodnight, then he was not the father to Jo he had promised he would be. He was no longer the dedicated husband he vowed on their wedding day. Jo and Emi would no longer be a Sanders but return to Grandeurs, despite how much her own father did not want her to speak, let alone carry his name.

On the final day, as Emi strolled around, as usual, she discovered a small park drenched in flowers of all sorts. Her favorites immediately caught her eye, and she stopped and sat on the bench, with her notebook and pen in hand. Without even thinking, she began to write. Her fingers led her pen in a dance around the page, and thoughts spilled out of her in an ever-flowing stream.

My Dearest Jo, the letter began.

Emi already missed her daughter's warm smile and outgoing presence. Jo's personality showed more through her actions and words every day, and Emi wondered if she had changed within this past week without her.

I would like you to know although I am away, I miss you terribly. I miss your billowing laugh, which fills my soul with glee, and I miss our dancing along to the record that spells how I feel for you: L.O.V.E.

I hope when I return, you and your father are well, and we are a family once again. I understand you are unaware now, but at times in your life, when you feel powerless and unloved, you must be the person to provide love within yourself. Never reach a place where you are not your own best caregiver because, as a woman, you are the only person you can confide in. You are my greatest blessing. I know as your mother, I have not been a great example of what a woman should be, but my wish for you is to go out into the world and become whoever you desire. You can do anything you set your mind to, and the world is bound to love you almost as much as I do.

I love you, darling, and this is something you can never forget because, no matter the distance between us, in body, mind, or soul, the love I feel for you can never be broken.

Love,
Your mother

Driving back after five days, a shorter trip than Emi had let on in her leaving home, she now knew she would return to a life she never envisioned for herself, in which family became a sole priority. Although she loved them as much as any mother could love their child, she recognized her life was one full of compromise.

As a child, Emi and her sisters would lay on their chilled marble floor beside the grand entrance, and they played with flimsy cornhusk dolls and discussed what they would be when they were older.

"When I'm older, I'm going to get married on a horse in a field. I will wear a diamond ring as big as the whole planet and brighter than all the stars," one of Emi's younger sisters said to her. Now, after years of Emi's absence, Emi had heard someone had granted her sister's wish. Her sister's ring was not as big as the whole planet, but it was much bigger than Emi's. Plus, Emi's family attended her sister's wedding, while their absence from hers proved devastating.

"When I'm older, I'm going to marry a doctor and become a nurse. I'll work at a brilliant hospital with patients whose days get even better as soon as they see me. And after that, I will have children, lots of them, and live on a great farm with chickens. I'll have a large garden with all of the most beautiful flowers in the world, with lots of dogwoods and my children's favorites because those will be the most beautiful."

Emi wanted to save lives and give more than she had received as a nurse with a great farm and beautiful garden with beautiful flowers. However, she was not a nurse, but she certainly gave more than she received.

Eyes heavy and arms trembling, Emi dreaded her discussion with Sonny. She wanted to talk with him and let him know she would get a job no matter what he felt was best for their family. Part of her wondered if he'd had a change of heart or if he was set in his ways.

As she walked inside, with her bag in hand and her legs shaking, Emi saw Sonny on the floor while he played with Jo and smiled.

"Emi?" Sonny gasped with excitement and immediately shifted from a look of relief to pure joy. "I'm so happy you're home." As he continued to play with Jo and provided Emi with more attention than he had in months, she realized this plan had worked, and he was beginning to have a change of heart.

That night, Emi lay in bed, wrapped in Sonny's arms, which she had nearly forgotten. Emi needed to follow through with the plan she had talked herself into for the entirety of her getaway. Although it did not feel like the right moment, she was unsure if there would ever be one.

"Sonny?" she whispered softly, unsure if he was awake or asleep. She knew if this could happen, it needed to happen now. From the gurgle of his throat and quick twitching of his hands, he was in limbo. He was saying farewell to sleep and beginning to regain full consciousness.

"Yes?" he said groggily, then moved his arms from under Emi's light body and rubbed his eyes awake.

"I'm going to get a job. Not as a nurse because I don't believe we can afford it, but as a store clerk or maybe even a secretary. I just need to do something, and that will happen no matter what you believe because I need to do it for myself."

"I didn't know you wanted to work that badly," he said, surprised, and his voice reached a higher pitch.

Her back turned to him, too nervous to see his reaction. She made it clear it was a statement, not a question.

"Okay. If that is what you want to do, then you should do it," he said.

Emi could sense his smile through his inflections without seeing his face.

Throughout the night, Emi stared at the eggshell-painted ceiling, and a feeling of nausea overwhelmed her. It was a poking sensation in the pit of her stomach, and it surrounded her skull. As she shifted, she searched for a more comfortable position. Unable to find one, a rushing wave of pain crashed over her, and Emi stood up as fast as she could. She rushed from the bedroom to the bathroom down the hall and released thin and heavily flowing vomit into the toilet. It consisted of nothing but water and the creamed corn she had eaten that day.

The last time Emi had vomited, she was pregnant with Jo. She lifted her face from the center of the toilet seat, then grabbed her stomach tightly, with both of her hands, and began to cry.

CHAPTER TEN

———

Emi vomited once in the morning and once in the evening, but she was unsure why. *Am I pregnant again?* After what she'd gone through, she'd hoped to begin her working career and do something for herself. But it seemed to have been for nothing.

After two weeks, she began to throw up at the sight of food, and chronic pains rose throughout her spine and aching skull. As a result, Emi went to the doctor. She did not tell Sonny of these symptoms, or the potential of this pregnancy, because she did not want him to worry or become too excited. It was not that Emi never wanted another child because she did, but the timing of this was wrong. Once she decided to work, she was unwilling to compromise. She wanted to truly live in lieu of focusing on everyone else's needs. It was not the right moment for Emi, but if she did try to do something to end this pregnancy, it would be the bitter end of their family. If Sonny ever found out, he would never be able to forgive her, and that was something she was unable to accept.

Sitting on the thin cover of translucent tissue paper on a doctor's table, lit under fluorescent lights, Emi waited. Her belly turned wildly within her, and her thin skin tingled in anticipation.

When the doctor arrived, he knocked first and strolled in wearing his astonishingly white coat. He smiled as if it had been the best news he had received all day, and he opened his mouth wide and said brightly. "It's your lucky day, Emi. You're pregnant and now pretty far along!"

Her head dropped and her body grew heavy. She believed she would lose all control and crash through the floor at any moment.

The doctor seemed startled. "Aren't you excited?" he questioned and stepped a bit closer to her, then placed his rough palm, with delicate long fingers, on her left shoulder.

"Yes, this is great," Emi said softly, then sniffled up mucus, which began to slowly drip through her nostrils. "I just wasn't expecting another pregnancy. The timing is a bit off."

"Well, the gift of a child is the greatest thing a woman receives. You should be grateful and look forward to a long life of cooking, cleaning, and being the best mother you can be." The doctor chuckled.

Emi rolled her eyes.

"Yes, of course, I am." Emi immediately thought of Sonny and how she would now need to prepare to become a mother of two and chain herself to the kitchen. Her only career would be *the housewife*.

———

Laying on their living room sofa, Emi watched an energized Jo run around her with one of her old rag dolls. Emi placed a frozen bag of peas to her heat-stricken forehead. Sonny walked in, crouched down low, and gave them both a soft peck on the cheek.

"What's the matter? Did you bump your noggin?" Sonny asked playfully and giggled.

As Emi pulled herself upright, Sonny's face changed from joy to concern.

"What is it? Are you alright?" he asked.

Emi nodded. She was unable to form the words and placed her hands within his, then pulled him closer. "I have something to tell you," Emi said apprehensively. "I–"

Sonny leaned in closer. He looked nervous, and his nostrils curled as they did whenever he showed intense focus. "Tell me," he said, unable to wait, and the tension built within the cramped room.

"I went to the doctor today, and I'm pregnant. I haven't been feeling well, so I went, and he gave me the news." She continued to hold his hands and looked away from Sonny immediately, too nervous about holding her eyes upon his face and awaiting.

Sonny stood up, grabbed Jo, and held her high into the air within the strength of his arms.

"I think this is the best news I've ever heard! I hope it's a boy!" He smiled, and Jo began to giggle with confusion, but she was pleased her father was happy.

Emi knew Sonny wanted a boy. She knew he wanted a child of his own blood so badly, and she was happy she would be able to give that to him.

"I'm happy you're happy." She joined the hug of Sonny and Jo and rested on his broad shoulder. Small tears trickled down her cheeks. Then, Emi turned her head away to hide her puzzling emotions. Emi was happy for Sonny, but she was not happy for herself.

The night, Sonny watched as Emi read a book, and he walked over, kissing her belly and blowing air into it to make tiny bubbling noises to make her laugh.

"This is great," he said and kissed Emi's stomach once again for good luck. "But there is something I think we should talk about."

"What's that?" Emi asked, but she already felt what he wanted to discuss. He knew about her excitement with work and the beginning of this new chapter.

"I know you said you feel the need to work," he said casually as he lay beside her. He looked slightly nervous but continued to stroke his burly fingers lightly across her belly in affection.

"What are you trying to say?" Emi asked.

As he breathed in a deep and unwieldy sigh, he braced for her disappointment, which he knew she was bound to exude, and began to speak again. "You know you can't get a job now, right? I mean, with two kids and all, it's going to be a lot of work. *We* need you home."

Emi knew this was true, of course. Her family needed her, and now, with another life to care for, this request was far from unreasonable.

"I know," she responded lightly and closed her book.

"I'm sorry, Em. I know how badly you wanted this, but I'm just thinking about our family." He extended his arm across Emi's waist, but her body remained settled. She did not pull away from Sonny's touch but did not embrace it either. *No matter how long it takes, I will live my dreams.* She looked away from Sonny and returned to her book.

PART TWO:

JO

CHAPTER ELEVEN

———

After Jo and Elaf dated for months, Elaf felt ready for her to immerse herself deeper into his community. Their connection sparked a desire within him to share her with others outside their inner circle, who would be honest in response to their unconventional college relationship.

"You should meet more of the women in the group," he said with a convincing smile that made Jo feel hesitant.

"Do you think they would want me there? I've never really met them before, and I don't know if they would like me all that much," Jo responded. She tensed her hands and looked up at his charming face.

"Don't worry," Elaf responded with a scoff. "They'll love you. Just go to the party tomorrow. You'll have fun."

———

As Jo arrived at a get-together consisting of all the women from Elaf's club, the mood shifted. After Jo walked through the door, women quickly adjusted their clothing to cover their faces before Jo could gaze upon them.

None of them trusted Jo, and that was clear as the bright light of a summer day. Although Jo had dated Elaf for six months, and everyone in his community knew who she was, they felt Jo was not to be trusted. They assumed she would spread the secrets of their physical appearance and womanly conversation amongst the club's men. It was awkward for them and for her. The tension grew as she roamed the crowded room as she introduced herself to strangers. Jo felt like an intruder in someone else's home.

She stayed for an hour and acted as if she enjoyed herself, only to return home when tensions became too high. She knew she could tell Elaf she'd tried, but as she left the party and walked down the steps onto the coarse pavement, she felt relief. The other women at the party came out from underneath their cherished cloth and re-exposed their faces as soon as she shut the door. Although she had known in her gut she would wind up isolated and unwelcome, it still hurt. Despite Elaf's clear desire for Jo's inclusion in his community, she felt this would never come to pass.

———

Jo and Elaf met in a bar in 1974. As Jo stumbled into the shadowy room, half-dazed, amidst thick cigarette smoke and the tinge of beer in her veins, she felt drawn to him instantly. Not only was he easy to spot because of his massive stature at six foot five inches, but if the prince of Aladdin were a real person, it would have been him. His dark brows and sharp cheekbones were striking, and to her surprise, his eyes were captivated by her as well. Perhaps he was drawn to her because she was the only Black person in that small town or because he found her beauty as enticing as she found his.

He slowly made his way toward Jo, and she welcomed him with acute flirtation.

"Hi, nice to meet you," he began, and he bent toward Jo slightly. They were unable to escape the ear-splitting sounds of the banging pool cues and the clinking of glass cups. He moved his ear closer to her lips and awaited a return to his brief introduction. When none was provided, he continued. "My name is Elaf. What's yours?"

"Hi, I'm Jo. Nice to meet you, too."

As they conversed about the surface level aspects of life, such as school and what brought them to a disgusting dive bar, Jo looked at him closely. She felt she had known him for far longer than an hour in the bustle of night. She gazed into his eyes, the closest to black Jo had ever seen, and desperately hoped the conversation would continue for hours or even days. The conversation flowed easily, and just from his voice, mannerisms, and the way he looked at her, she could tell this would develop into something more. She did not want this person to slip from her grasp when their attraction had felt so effortless. He felt the same.

"It's getting pretty late." Jo leaned on the bar counter and looked down at their drinks to count. Jo had one lemon drop and two shots of vodka, and Elaf had two light beers and one whiskey shot, which he'd downed solely to impress her.

"Yeah, it is," Elaf looked around the room to see if there were any other activities for them to fill the time, but he only saw people slowly leaving. The room lacked energy, and all who remained were in the process of throwing in the towel and calling it a night.

"I know this is a little crazy, but do you want to come to my place? We can talk a little more if that sounds fun to you. I've really liked getting to know you, Jo."

"Sure, that sounds fun," Jo responded hesitantly. She lifted the curls of her lips slightly, and her stomach felt jittery.

His apartment was dark and dingy, and it was clear he was not the only twenty-something-year-old man who laid their head in this space at night. Jo and Elaf laid on a mattress that provided no support whatsoever. This was an experience she was bound to have at some point in her life. It was crucial to meet new people and stretch her wings beyond her comfort zone.

She woke to the warmth of his golden skin. It felt like more than a one-night stand. They were inseparable from that day forward, and both knew it as they whispered their first goodnight.

With Elaf still in school, he spent most of his time with his friends in a club, which consisted of Saudi Arabian students. Elaf attended an American school on exchange. He planned to return to his family sometime but did not know when. Because Jo had never dated anyone outside the culture of Black or White, this was new for her, especially since Elaf had an entire life in another country that did not include her. She was surrounded by his friends constantly. There were many things Jo learned, and she was often the only woman, the only one who could show her face. It was simply not a part of their culture to spend these intimate gatherings with Saudi women. This rule was only broken with marriage.

The only other woman Jo saw around was the wife of one of Elaf's friends. She was a girl from this small conservative town, though she was disowned by her family when she dated the man who became her husband. In her marriage, she morphed herself into a traditional Muslim wife, both out of want and the belief there was no other option. She was close to iridescent, and she shone under the beautiful lavender fabrics that hung around her head and covered her frosty blond hair. Jo never really talked to her when she was at their house because she kept busy and prepared food for the men to devour. They sat on old newspapers atop the splintered wooden floor, and they chowed down on every meal.

Jo examined this woman who seemed happy at times but sad in the presence of others. For Jo, it was intimidating to see this woman's commitment and what she gave up. *Could I do this?* Jo asked herself as she watched the woman return to the kitchen as she had been ordered to do. Jo knew her family would accept Elaf, as they always had open minds and hearts, but she was unsure if this shift of culture would prove overwhelming.

Jo's life became a mindless routine, and the fear of this worsening terrified her. She worked for a small fashion magazine in a town that was not fashion-forward and spent time with Elaf and his friends whenever her schedule would allow. She lived in Spokane, Washington. It was far enough away from home to feel as though she was on her own but close enough to return when need be. Spokane was a place fit for those who enjoyed a quiet life. Jo had had big dreams since before she could remember, and she'd envisioned New York City or Los Angeles instead of this mountainous place where only farmers seemed to thrive, and college students drowned their stresses and sorrows in cheap beer and tequila. While Elaf still had two more years of school left and had made plans to go to graduate school just hours away, Jo knew she had to keep her options open and not commit to a life she felt unsure of at such a young age.

Her dream of being a fashion editor showed its face when she picked up her first magazine. As she admired the beautiful faces on the cover, she looked up at her from her mother's dresser with a serious expression, feeling inspired. Jo had loved clothes all her life. Wearing designer brands was always a dream, which she had not yet achieved, and she longed to make her own clothes one day, to emulate the sparks of genius seen in the pages of *Mademoiselle* and *Vogue*.

When she peered into the future after high school graduation, she saw herself in a big place doing big things. She never envisioned a start-up in a small town, just a few hours from home, but that is life. Jo knew she had to take little steps to make sure she was on the right path to arrive at the big destination, and New York City was *her* big destination.

CHAPTER TWELVE

———

Jo broke the seal of an envelope she had been patiently waiting to receive for weeks. She could not have been more delighted her dream to move to New York was finally becoming a reality. Her mind was consumed with endless planning and pondering what she would pack and where she would live. The biggest thing that weighed on her mind was how she would break the bittersweet news to Elaf, who planned to stay in Washington until he finished school and possibly after.

As she sat across from him in the hole-in-the-wall diner they had become familiar with through many dates, they stared at one another blankly. They recognized the brutal silence between them, and Jo was the only one who held the answer to why it was there in the first place.

"So, I have something to tell you," she stated in an insecure tone as Elaf chewed the last bite of his hamburger.

He wiped the greased corners of his mouth and smiled, intrigued and free of worry, aside from confusion.

"You know how I've wanted to move to New York for a really long time? Well, I got a job there working as an assistant for a fashion editor, and I decided to take it."

The lined corners of his mouth dropped from a grin to a look of anguish. Jo knew this was a decision she would probably never be forgiven for. It was the ultimate dagger to the heart since she'd deceived him by withholding such crucial information, though, at this time, she did not see it as such.

"Why didn't you ask me if it was okay?" he asked in a stern tone.

She was taken aback by his question. They were not married, and this was something she had wanted long before she stepped into that bar and set her eyes on him for the first time months ago.

Showing no mercy, Elaf began to shout, which drew the attention of the entire diner and brought the buzzing of anxiousness to life in Jo's body. Her heart pounded more rapidly, and her temples ached in concern.

"We are supposed to be together. You are supposed to be my wife after I graduate, and now you just decide to abandon me?"

Elaf rose from his seat and stood over Jo's seated form. He looked furious as if smoke came through his ears and flames through his eyes. He shouted so robustly Jo could not stand to stay in the situation any longer.

"I can't believe you would do this to me!" he continued, then bent farther down, close enough to her face she could feel his warm breath that smelled of beef and mustard.

Looking around, all she could see were the eyes of strangers who wanted to help but seemed afraid. Jo turned back toward Elaf, who still managed to have enough air in his lungs to continue his rage-filled speech. She pushed past him, then charged out of the restaurant as if to run for her life. Jo felt the tightening of her chest as the abounding eyes trailed her out of the door, and Elaf marched quickly behind her as he yelled.

Strangers felt sorry for this girl they did not know in what seemed like an undesirable situation, but they did nothing to address it.

———

Pieces of clothing were scattered around the floor, and with only a few hours until Jo would move from a drab little town to the big city, she had a lot of packing to do. As she folded each shirt with delicacy and pristine organization, she heard knocks on the door. They were so light and reserved she had a feeling it would be someone who was afraid to see her. There was only one person who had any reason to be fearful. Cracking the door slightly, she saw the big stature of this scared man. Jo immediately dreaded what was to come and knew it would be anything but a peaceful interaction.

"I'm really sorry, Jo. Can I please come in?" Elaf asked, showing nothing but his eyes and nose through the opening of the door.

Jo reluctantly opened it and let him inside.

"I'm so sorry, Jo," he began again, then walked through the thin entryway of her old home and trailed Jo as she quickly returned to her room to pack her things. "I didn't mean to embarrass you or make a scene on our date, but I was really angry. I was hoping that maybe we could talk about it now and see if there is any way you could find it in your heart to stay. *For me.*"

"What about *for me*, Elaf?" Jo snapped as she turned to face him quickly, and her frustration fueled her words. "I've done so many things you've wanted me to do. I always hung out with *your* friends, and I tried being friends with all the girls you know because you wanted me to, even though I knew they hated me. I always did everything for *you*, but now it's time for that to be enough. This has been my dream forever, and I am not throwing that away for someone who clearly cares more about what is in his best interest than someone he claims to love and want to marry."

"If you want to. Nobody's going to force you to do anything, but I just don't understand why you would do this. I mean, we've been moving toward joining our lives together. We were supposed to get married, and now, because you are deciding to be selfish, I have to go back home. My mom will force me to get an arranged marriage because you won't bother to stay around. You are ruining my life, and you don't even care!"

As this left his lips, regret quickly followed, immediate and forceful, but then he felt anger.

"You know what I am?" he went on, and he followed Jo as she began to leave.

Her face looked numb, and she zipped her bags rapidly, then grabbed them as she headed for the door.

"I am a different breed of man, and you are going to wish you never left for that stupid assistant job you call a dream!"

When Jo walked down her creaky porch steps and into the fresh air, Elaf continued to trail behind her, and he only grew louder with his hateful words.

"Jo, come back here! You need to stay! I can't believe you are doing this to us!"

Once Jo reached her car, she no longer paid Elaf any mind. His loud yells turned hollow and inaudible. With the final shutting of her trunk, she felt her life fall in order and was ready to be transported to what seemed like another world.

She looked back at the man who trailed her, and for a brief moment, she giggled in amusement.

"Just take the spare key under the mat and lock the house up for me!" she shouted across the street happily. "There are going to be some new people moving in tomorrow, so just make sure everything is in order, okay? Maybe you can trap one of them into marrying you," she laughed.

Elaf grew red. "You are going to miss me when I am gone, Jo Sanders, just you wait and see! You are going to be crawling back within a week. I bet you."

"Yeah, I'm sure I will, Elaf," Jo barked, then got into her car and drove away. She left Elaf in his cloud of misery as she burst out with laughter, relieved at her escape from that life.

CHAPTER THIRTEEN

———

Jo never felt happier than when she went on coffee runs and hoped one day, she would sit in one of the head editors' seats and make life-altering decisions for the benefit of fashion.

Although she was consumed by work and dreams of where the city would take her, one element of Jo's personal life that seemed to be trapped in a slump, after Elaf, was love. Jo was unsure what her connection with Elaf really was, but she knew the dates she had in the city were no better than the experiences back at home. The butterflies in her stomach had not been resurrected since their separation.

Despite the fact she had not found anyone worthwhile in this foreign place, Jo felt happy to be independent and live a life that did not need to be altered for the benefit of anyone other than herself. She was excited to go out whenever she pleased, meet new people, and live guilt-free. She did not have to worry about bringing anyone down or them doing the same to her.

She had lived this new life for just over two months, and there had not been a week when Elaf did not call. Living in a microscopic apartment that held dust at every corner, Jo would constantly wake to the blaring ring of her phone at all hours of the night. She answered every call to put the ear-splitting rings to an end, but she knew she would be faced with an angry or pathetic voice on the other side.

"I can't live without you," Elaf droned on one late night. "Please, Jo. My parents are making me return home and get married. If somewhere in your heart you believe we still have a chance, then come home. Save me. *I still love you.*"

"Elaf, I have told you so many times I'm not coming back. It's not going to work, and I'm sorry, but you just need to stop doing this," Jo responded, then lay the side of her head on her silk-lined pillow. The phone rested on her ear, and her deep eyes shone their flecks of green in the blue night. She was barely able to keep her eyes open, but the burning in her chest and temples continued as he kept talking.

"You know what?" he began again, feeling a bit more fired up by Jo's new lack of interest. "Fine. Have a nice life, and I *will* get married. I'm just glad it won't be to you."

Although the last conversation ended in spite and disinterest on Elaf's end, Jo continued to receive these calls from him. He said the same things that, after a while, felt more in the form of a proposition or request rather than an overdone declaration of profound love. She pressed the phone up to her ear, the bottom half tucked between her shoulder and the pit of her neck for countless nights, after Jo had spent time with friends or escaped from an incredibly awkward date.

She would tell Elaf once again she no longer felt the same. "I can't come back, Elaf. I'm living a whole new life out here, and it's everything I've ever wanted. I'm sorry, but it's really over. It would be best for both of us if you just finally move on. I have."

In actuality, Jo was not sorry at all. Of course, she felt bad for the situation his parents had put him in, but she would not sacrifice her lifelong hopes, dreams, and desires to move back home just to marry Elaf and become a traditional Muslim wife. She knew she had not loved him enough to make such a drastic change. It might have worked for the girl she had become accustomed to seeing on their college nights, with her bright white skin that shone through the vibrant fabrics, as she prepared a full meal and never looked Jo in the eye. She seemed tolerant of her life, and perhaps she genuinely enjoyed it, but Jo knew was not the life *she* wanted.

———

As Jo established her necessary role in the editorial world, the last place she thought she would be was home. Not home as in college or Elaf, but in the house she had grown up in. It contained people she loved the most in this world but had not seen and struggled to keep in contact with since graduation.

Deep into the night, Jo's phone's sporadic ring provoked a shiver down her spine. She felt her stomach automatically twist with stress that Elaf had gone back on his rampage of phone calls and pathetic propositions. When she finally sat up, she took out her knotted scrunchie and rewrapped her deep brown strands in their secure bun, she answered the phone and braced for Elaf's voice, but to her surprise, it was a different man's tone. It was her younger brother, Milo.

"Joey, you there?" he said quickly, and the stress in his voice projected.

"Milo? What's up? Why are you calling so late?"

Judging by his long pause after her question, she knew something was wrong. She could only hear Milo's breathing through the speaker, and it grew a bit faster as the silence amplified.

"Jo, I'm sorry to spring this on you because I've heard from Ma everything with you has been going great, but it's Dad. She says he'll probably be fine, but he's getting pretty sick, and I know you haven't seen him in a while, so I thought I should give you the invite to come back just for a week or two, to spend time with us if you can."

Jo spoke with Milo for a while, and they discussed the stresses of their father's health and Milo's high school. After they spoke, Jo realized how much she missed Milo. She did not realize how much she missed her whole family until that call. As she heard his voice and his excitement as they discussed his loves, losses, and mistakes, Jo wished she could be there to see Milo change from a boy to a man. He told her he appeared in every paper in the state for his athletic achievements. She had missed out on more than she had thought, and as he continued, she noticed his voice had dropped even lower since their last conversation. A hole formed in her heart, which only the rest of the Sanders' family could fill.

"I have to get time off of work, and I'm not sure I can, but I'll see what I can do," she said in a reassuring voice.

"Okay, good. We all miss you, Joey. It's like you don't even think about your family anymore."

Remaining on the line, Jo lay still in her bed, drenched in the sound of silence. She knew Milo was right. She did not think about her family nearly as much as she should, especially since the big move.

"I know, buddy. Tell you what, I'll be home in a few days. I'll make it work. I promise."

CHAPTER FOURTEEN

———

As Jo sat in the taxi as it drove around the corner, she looked through the window, and she saw the simple old hunk of white bricks she knew well. As she opened the car door and was handed her bags, she could see Milo through the window. He flashed a smile, and his bright gums shined through the deep tones of his lips and richly pigmented skin. Jo opened the door and stepped inside, to see her mother as she hummed Nat King Cole on her new record player and frosted a cake. Jo guessed the cake was for her father because it was covered in dazzling yellow suns. Looking back at all the times her parents were at their best, Jo felt her mother's favorite thing about her father was his name.

"Sonny!" Jo's mother said as she walked over to him almost every morning when Jo was a child. She always hugged Sonny from behind as he ate his morning breakfast before he headed out to work. "With your name and my eyes, we could brighten up the whole house. Scratch that; the whole world!" she'd say lightly.

Sonny would cackle and return the embrace with a grateful expression. He knew his wife loved him just as much as he loved her. His name resembled who he was: a man who brightened up the room and sky as soon as he stepped foot in it, and he always showed everyone around him how great a man could truly be.

As Jo greeted her mother and brother, she could tell they were both surprised she had actually come to visit. She was able to drop everything and leave her new life in order to return to the old.

"Why aren't you back at your job in New York?" her mother asked with an inquisitive gaze. She rubbed her thin pale fingers on a kitchen towel to relieve them of the crystalized residue and gave Jo a big hug before she could respond.

"Well, Ma, I actually called Jo and told her she should come to visit because of Dad," Milo admitted. Her father was sick with the possibility of no recovery.

Jo entered her father's bedroom, with its pink pastel curtains drawn and a creaky fan that blew in the direction of his face. He was sprawled across the entirety of the bed and fast asleep, and he snored steadily. As Jo sat next to him, she placed her hand on his forehead, and she transferred beads of sweat to the insides of her fingers and in the crack between the band of her rings and the skin of her pinky. He opened his midnight eyes and flashed a smile, which he had gifted Milo at birth.

"My Joey," he said, hardly able to get the words out from his raw throat. "Why are you here? You should be in your fancy job in New York." He began, then looked into Jo's eyes, which were already welling with tears. "It's just pneumonia, ya know. A couple more days, and I'll be back to normal. I promise."

Jo's hand was still on his forehead and moved up, then stroked through his short salt and pepper coils, which now extended from his sideburns to an impressively coarse beard.

They talked for a while about her decision to leave Washington to move to New York and how she was with her newfound independence. Looking at him in his helpless state, she was unaware of her mother's surprise that awaited him in the kitchen. It didn't occur to Jo how much she needed him. She loved not only her father but her mother and Milo as well. She had a family that so many dream of, so why on Earth did she decide to move across the country and leave them behind?

———

After a week of being at home, her father made a full recovery as promised. Meanwhile, it was nice for Jo to take a break from the busy city life she had grown accustomed to and return to her family where she was raised. As Milo became older, he moved toward high school graduation and looked at possible scholarships for track and field. As he grew up, change was all around, and Jo decided to extend her stay for another week to catch up with those she left after graduation. Even though it was not ideal, and her boss was less than pleased with her extended stay, she had managed to squeeze one last week for herself.

One friend Jo had not seen for years but missed constantly was Johnny Jefferson. When they entered college freshman year and locked eyes, it was as if, at that moment, they each knew they would be best friends all the way up to graduation. Johnny was a quiet soul whose inner extrovert popped out after a few drinks. He loved the concept of love and wanted it for everyone around him but himself.

"I'll set you up with any of my friends. You just take your pick!" he would tell Jo. He sat on the carpeted floor of her dorm room after they went out for the night and were not quite in the mood for sleeping but instead stuffed their faces with the cheapest cheese pizza they could find, then slurped leaky boxes of wine.

Although she had respectfully declined all his offers ever since she left school, she was single for the first time in a while, and she arranged to go out with Johnny while she was home. She was ecstatic about all the possibilities his match-making skills would provide. Suddenly, these arrangements would not be against her will.

After a day of cooking with her mother, watching Western films with her father, and playing basketball in the front yard with her brother, Jo was due for time away, so she spent it with the friend she had missed most.

As Johnny pulled into the driveway, he avoided the ancient cracks in the pavement and made his best attempt not to scratch his new Ford Cortina on the rogue evergreen branches. He was eager to show Jo all the new friends he had made and the new places he had discovered since he finished school.

After Johnny knocked on the door, he waited on the porch with his hands crossed behind his back as if anxiously antic-ipating a first date.

Jo's mother opened the door, and her face lit up with the organic joy only Johnny could coax out of her.

"Hey, Mrs. Sanders. Long time no see!" Johnny said as she embraced him, then pulled him into the house and eagerly showed him off to the rest of the family.

"Look, it's Johnny Jefferson!" she exclaimed to Sonny and Milo. "Johnny, you have no idea how much we've missed having you around the house in Jo's old college days. How've you been?"

"You know, the usual. I've been working to pay the bills and helping the old man whenever he needs me. I'm glad Jo is back in town for a little while, though. We haven't spent time together in a long while."

"Don't I know it. You know, I always thought the two of you would end up together. How wild is that?"

"Yeah," Johnny chuckled under his breath. "Love isn't really for me I don't think but if I can find it for her with one of my pals, I'll let you know."

Jo's mother chuckled in response.

"Okay, the two of you, no talking about me," Jo quickly said as she stepped out of her bedroom door. She knew when her mother and Johnny were together, no good ever came of it.

"Oh, you know, Joey. Whenever I'm over here, we always have to talk about you behind your back just a little bit," Johnny laughed.

Jo walked up to him quickly and pulled him through the door.

As they slipped away, Johnny hurriedly waved goodbye to the family he was dragged away from. "Bye, Sanders' fam! See all y'all soon, I hope."

"Bye, Johnny!" Jo's mother said as she smiled at Jo's joking annoyance. "You know you are welcome in this house anytime."

As they strolled into an overpacked club later that night, the stench of vodka and citrus swirled through the air. After a long wait in the bitter cold, Johnny and Jo were more than ready to knock down a few shots and make this night one to remember.

As Jo drank, danced, and met a few of Johnny's new friends, she noticed this was not the same Johnny she had once known. Now, he was a version that seemed to have shown an interest in bettering himself by limiting his alcohol intake at least at the beginning of the night. Jo watched him across the room as he chatted with his friends and remained calm and collected as he did when he was sober. This differed from his once destructive drunk self. He seemed to possess responsibility and maturity while maintaining his love for a good time, which she wished he developed in their college days. While it seemed like he only held a drink for appearance amongst the group, he began to take sips here and there, and with every one, Jo's heart sank.

In school, Johnny's only agenda was to have fun and avoid anything that got in the way of it. Smoking, drinking, and partying were his only plans, and after a while, he slowly began to spiral into a handful of bad habits.

Although Jo loved Johnny with everything she had inside of her, their third year tested their friendship. Even though Jo liked to party at times, even drank and smoked when she felt in the mood, Johnny would do it every day. He even used cocaine and harder substances Jo could never get behind or understand. He always reached for the rush of feeling the best he ever had. He had a knack for finding the people who felt the same, who only held ambitions to stay young forever and high through it all.

One evening, when Jo went to a party with Johnny and a few of his questionable friends, Johnny dug himself deep into a haze of confusion and numbness he could not escape. He ended that night laying on a bathroom floor with puke spread all around him. His friends left him behind to fend for himself, probably in the hopes Jo or a random person would find him through all the chaos.

He remained there for hours, and his body vibrated from the music. He sunk into the floor, and no one came into the bathroom to discover him. He was unconscious, unaware of just how vulnerable he was in a place that was supposed to be lighthearted. His peers were in the very same house one floor down and experienced a completely different life. They did not worry about reaching such a low as Johnny had.

"Johnny?" Jo gasped as she walked into the bathroom. She had searched for him for half an hour by then and began to think he and his friends had left her behind. She had already planned the speech she would give him tomorrow morning about what a bad friend he had become.

"Johnny, get up!" she screamed, then crouched next to his body, which rose and fell with his shallow breath. "Someone help!" She began to yell, harder and harder, with each phrase. The music blared through the record player and over her high-pitched voice, which began to fail.

"Johnny, get up!" Jo yelled again, then pumped his chest as hard as she could. She knew he was breathing but tried to gather all the information she had learned in her CPR certification back in the early years of high school. She placed her lips to his thin blue ones and blew air into his mouth while she continued to pump his body with all she had. She didn't know what else to do. "Someone help!"

As she continued to push and blow all the air from her lungs into his, Johnny woke up with a cough. His milky blue eyes barely opened, and his ghostly pale face grew as red as a ripe summer cherry.

"Jo?" he said softly, then stared up at her as she cried harder now. Her head leaned down into his neck, and his hand reached inside of her thick dark hair. "Hey, it's okay. I'm fine, really. I don't know what happened. I probably just drank a little too much." He looked around and flinched at all the bodily liquids around him. He had not known they had all come from him.

"Johnny, you need to stop," Jo continued to hug him, unfazed by what was around her. "I can't be friends with you anymore if you're like this. You can't be this person. You just can't."

"Okay," Johnny responded, and his voice cracked in embarrassment and shame. "I'm sorry, Joey. I'm really sorry. I'll stop."

———

As Jo was drowned with introductions, Johnny did not push any of his friends on her but stated he had a surprise at the end of the night.

"Trust me, Jo. I have something that will make this night one of both nostalgia and new memories."

While this did excite her, it made the pit of her stomach swirl carrying bits of nervousness and anxiety.

At the end of the night, Jo and Johnny walked back to his apartment, and his lean arms were wrapped around Jo's neck and tugged on the loose bun at the back of it. The surprise Johnny had blabbed to her about all night would have to be postponed, and Jo was slightly disappointed a night with him had resulted in this outcome once again. He had drunk one too many and was now wasted beyond belief, with Jo as his only saving grace. He trudged up the narrow staircase outside and through the door of his muggy city apartment as he swayed in and out of consciousness.

"You know, I don't usually drink like this anymore," he said, beginning to defend himself from the judgment he knew Jo held. "Just place me on the floor here, and I'll be fine. My carpet is really soft, so I'll be comfortable."

As he laid down, he pressed his shoulder into the stained oatmeal carpet, intertwined with loose strands of his light blond waves and crumbs from mystery meals. Johnny lifted his head and opened his eyes wide, which caused Jo to flinch with a flash of surprise as she began to doze off in the chair beside him.

"Are you ready for my surprise?" he asked, and his voice wavered.

"Yeah, sure," Jo chuckled sleepily as he managed to stand up and pull out a movie he had kept in his unorganized bookcase.

"I give you... *Love Story*," he said and held up two movie tickets and waved them in the air excitedly. Jo smiled from ear to ear at how sweet this was of Johnny to want to watch this with her. It had been their favorite film in college.

"How did you know when it's playing?" she asked.

As she got up out of the sinking leather seat and walked toward his swaying body to hug him, he held up his finger and slurred words with a concentrated effort to form them into a coherent sentence.

"My buddy works at the theatre and told me the film was being shown for this weekend only. But..." he spit out messily. "If we go see this tomorrow, then you have to do something for *me*."

Jo crossed her arms tightly, and her smile turned into a look of suspicion.

"You need to let me give your number to this friend of mine."

"Johnny, really?" Jo sighed in disappointment, as she always did at his outrageous matchmaking proposals.

"Joey, come on. He's a really great guy, and I knew him from Sunday school back when we were kids. I told him about you, and he said he wants to talk with you, so can you just do it? Please?"

They went back and forth for a while, and Jo tried to convince him she did not want to be set up with anyone.

Johnny gently pulled her down to sit beside him on the floor. "Listen. I know you don't want me to set you up, but this guy would be great with you. In college, I was just messing around, but he is actually the real deal. Just give it a shot for your old pal Johnny."

"Fine. He can just have my phone number, but that's it. That doesn't mean anything is going to happen."

Johnny began to smile now, still wobbly from the alcohol content in his body, and he wrapped his arms around Jo. He placed his head on her shoulder endearingly, "You won't regret it. Now, are you ready to cry watching this movie or what?"

CHAPTER FIFTEEN

———

Jo spent her time perfecting pastry icing techniques with her mother and discovering which old country songs her father liked now. She found she had reached the age where she was still treated as their daughter but no longer a person they had cared for. She was left alone to do what she wished and go where she pleased at any time of night, but when left alone with either of them or both, they treated her as an equal. They poured large glasses of whiskey and asked if she wanted to sit and watch the game, or better yet, a romance film on the television, which was her mother's favorite pastime and now her father's, by association.

In the midst of their casual conversations about life and where Jo believed she was headed in her career, her mother initiated a topic she could never escape. She asked for an update on Jo's relationship status. Jo had experiences in high school, which now seemed incredibly insignificant, and the pattern had carried on throughout college, apart from Elaf. Her mother was never satisfied with the short answers Jo said she had dated every now and again, but none of the men had ever appeared special enough to hold onto for long.

"You don't need someone *special*," her mother would always say in her calm voice. She broke her eyes from the television screen and anxiously carried on the conversation, with the knowledge she could miss something crucial. "You just need *someone*."

Even though Jo's father had no problem with her taking as much time as she needed and even dying alone if she saw fit, her mother was passionate about the matter. She wanted Jo to find someone not only to have kids and grow old with but to be a companion and a form of support through the most difficult times.

"You know, when I met your father, he didn't have to be with me or take care of you, but he did. He looked at me and said this was what he wanted, and I knew. He would not only be my husband, but he would be my friend, my partner for *life,* and the father of a child that didn't even share his own blood."

Although Jo admired her father beyond belief and wished it was that easy for her to find a soul mate of her own, she'd never experienced that. She had never looked at someone and knew that person was one she would feel not only comfortable with but excited to spend the rest of her life with. It seemed not only unlikely but impossible, and Jo had already told herself if she were to die alone and never have children, she would have to learn to be okay with that. She'd learned not to resent herself or her inability to find true love, as it was rare, and most people never do.

———

Jo took small sips of lukewarm whiskey and watched her father yell at a football game on television, which was entirely uninteresting. She had not heard from Johnny in a few days and had begun to feel as though he had slipped back into his old life when she was not around. Maybe he was preparing for Jo's departure the following week and did not want to relive the heartbreaking goodbye they'd had at graduation.

With the days passing by, Jo began to rethink the life she had chosen for herself in New York. She was once again getting used to the clean air in Washington. She enjoyed the evergreen and maple trees that shaded her at all times and the quiet. Here, she only heard birds chirp and hummingbirds flutter their wings in the cool mornings, which brought her joy, with the light clicking of raindrops against her windowsill at night. It could not be more different from city life. It was a community where everyone knew one another, and no one was able to walk past a store or a familiar face without asking them about their day and how much their children or siblings had grown since they last saw them. Although Jo had begun to resent this culture and felt she was now above it, she did not know if she wanted to leave it all behind just yet, or at all, really. *Am I ready for New York?* She knew she was because of how she had adapted in the short months. *Do I want to live in New York?* That was the real question Jo had never truly thought about. She felt she could not because of the career she pursued.

These internal thoughts ran through her mind as the whiskey began to make a noticeable appearance in her brain and body. It caused heat to trap inside the top layer of her skin. Jo's father continued to yell at the screen now as he stood. He waved his arms repeatedly up into the air as she watched the game mindlessly.

Sitting groggily, Jo perked up with surprise as the phone rang on the wall. As her mother placed her knife on the counter and wiped her hands from the stickiness of peeled apples, she answered the phone. She first showed confusion but quickly changed to brimming excitement.

"Joey, it's for you." She smiled ear to ear as Jo walked up and grabbed the phone from her. Jo untangled the curling telephone wire around her mother's arm to relieve her from it and heard an innocent voice that contained deep tones and an aura of shy confidence.

"Jo Sanders?" he asked, a bit nervous. "This is Raymond Woodson. I don't know if Johnny asked you or told you, but he gave me your phone number, and I just thought I would call to introduce myself and say he has told me a lot of great things about you."

Heart beating faster and limbs feeling as if they were electrocuted, Jo was unsure what to expect from this mystery man Johnny had advocated so hard for. He sounded sweet, and by the tone of his voice, she imagined he probably was not bad looking either.

"Yeah, that's me. Johnny did mention you," Jo said with a chuckle, and she heard a laugh from Raymond on the opposite line. "But I don't really know much about you, I have to admit."

"Of course," Raymond responded, and the pitch of his voice perked up the minute Jo showed interest. "Where would you like me to start?"

———

Feeling her knees begin to buckle from over an hour of conversation, Jo sat on the floor under the kitchen counter and talked and laughed harder than she had since she could remember. Their easy-flowing conversation felt as if it was pulled from thin air but organized itself seamlessly. Jo talked for a while, and she watched her mother continue to prepare her apple pie. She knew full well her mother was eavesdropping. Her mother tried not to reveal her smile.

"Well, it was great talking to you, Jo. I have to get to bed because I have work in the morning, but I would love to talk to you again sometime," Raymond said. All the nerves in his voice from before had dissipated to reveal only silkiness in his tone.

"Okay, sounds great. Talk to you soon," Jo responded and hung up, then relieved her neck from the crooked position it had molded into after all that time.

Jo's mother turned around in a state of disbelief as soon as the phone returned on the wall.

"So, who was *that*?" she asked, convinced by Jo's dislike of discussing love that she was not interested in dating. Now, she was more intrigued than ever.

"I don't know," Jo paused awkwardly, then looked down at the floor and grinned to herself. "But I think I'm going to marry him." Once she said this, her mother broke into laughter, then bent over and began to snort puffs of air and make noises that should rather be coming out of a farm animal. Quickly, she settled down once she realized the sincerity of her statement.

"Well, we'll see, won't we?" she whispered to Jo, then kissed her cheek and returned to her pie. "I'm just glad you want to get married at all."

CHAPTER SIXTEEN

———

Thinking back to her first phone call with Raymond, Jo had never dreamed of a connection as effortless as this. It was difficult for Jo to believe they had now dated for just over six months, and both felt as strongly for one another as they had in their first encounter. He was tall, stylish, and attractive like Jo desperately hoped he would be, and then, they discovered their personalities were entirely different but complemented each other.

"Hi Jo, it's nice to finally see you," Raymond said the first time they met just a week after their first phone call. His demeanor quiet and reserved. He hugged Jo gently as soon as he climbed out of his car. He stood in front of her house with plans to take her to one of his favorite restaurants in the city.

"Hi, nice to see you too," Jo responded eagerly as she attempted to suck in her excitement. She was overwhelmed by how he had already exceeded her expectations with a simple greeting.

Valentine's Day had been around the corner, and both Jo and her mother had the feeling something special would take place. "You know what *I* think?" her mother said in the voice she used when she gossiped with her friends or Jo's father.

"He is going to propose. There's no way it's not happening on Valentine's Day!"

Jo acted as if she did not think he would propose, but she secretly hoped he would. She was excited by how giddy her mother had been about the whole situation and about Raymond himself. Although her mother had met a few of Jo's other boyfriends, she had not liked them nearly as much as Raymond. "He's a doctor, he's Black, and he loves his mother. What more could you want?" she always said when she described him to family members or friends who asked about how Jo was, though they usually had no actual interest in the intricacies of Jo's love life. For Jo, it felt good to have someone. Convinced just months ago, she would never find anyone at all, and now this man stood before her with the possibility of taking her hand in marriage in just a few short days.

———

On the day Jo and her mother had eagerly awaited, Jo had never been more excited to go to work, just so she could finish her shift to go on the dinner date Raymond had set up for them. As Jo worked her new, temporary job as a waitress in a disco club to make money as she looked for magazine opportunities closer to her old home, she learned to enjoy the art of customer service. She even developed quite an act for carrying trays packed with food on roller skates and remembered the orders of the regulars by heart.

Rolling past all the holiday decorations set up on this day of love, Jo was in a good mood. She was consumed with thoughts of Raymond and fantasized about how her left hand would look with an engagement ring on it. As she spoke to customers happily, she rolled around and danced to music, and she sang along to the new works of Gloria Gaynor.

"Hey, Jo! There's a call for you," one of her coworkers barked, then cupped the bottom of the telephone with her hand to block the outside noise and wag her eyebrows in intrigue.

As Jo walked over, she considered how strange it was to receive a phone call at work, but she picked up the phone. "This is, Jo. Who's calling?"

"It's Elaf, *remember me?*" said the voice of a man she thought had vacated her life for good.

Jo quickly felt cold and wished she did not remember him at all.

"So," he said matter of factly, "long story short, I officially divorced my wife, and I heard you moved back home, so I'm coming back to Washington to see you. What do you think of *that?*" he said assuredly, more excited than he should be.

Jo was frozen in astonishment. The call was so random after not having spoken to him for almost a year. She stayed on the line and listened to his hollow words. She could tell by the confidence in his tone he believed he would win her back, but the possibility of that happening was nonexistent.

"I'm sorry, Elaf, but we ended a long time ago. I have a boyfriend now, so I can't see you."

"Well, just blow him off. I'm coming all the way to see you, and you're not even going to let me take you out for Valentine's Day?" He chuckled on the brink of breaking into a pathetic whine.

As she continued to listen to his tactics to make her feel bad or guilty, Jo reached the point where she'd had enough. "Listen, I'm sorry you had to get an arranged marriage and left your wife, but it's not really my problem. You just need to let it go."

The phone clanked against the restaurant wall as she quickly hung up. At this point, she did not care what response Elaf had in store for her blunt reply. Jo returned to work. Her legs shook, but she pretended their conversation never happened and promised herself it would remain private.

————

Raymond's face glowed in the candlelight as Jo leaned her arms across the smooth silk of the tablecloth. They talked casually and ate dinner as if it was any other night out.

"How was your day at work?" he asked.

With no desire to tell Raymond of her call with Elaf or who Elaf even was, she gave a vague response. "Oh, you know. Just the same as always. What about you?"

The waitress put down her tiramisu and Raymond's bananas foster as she began to feel a shadow of doubt. Did he have plans to propose, or was it a figment of her mother's imagination? Feeling bliss with every bite of dessert she took, she noticed Raymond seemed filled with indecisiveness.

"Are you alright?" she asked, and her lips slightly stuck together from the cream and coffee filling. Raymond sat up straight and dug into his jacket pocket. What was supposed to be discreet immediately made her heart drop to her stomach.

Looking at his hands with intense focus, Jo saw he gently cupped a small velvet green box and quickly ducked it under the table.

"Sorry, I'm a little shaky," he said nervously, with his voice quiet so as not to draw attention. "Jo, I love you. You know that," he began, then leaned across the table to get closer to her face. "And I've been thinking a lot about us and what the future holds. When I think about it, and what I see, it's always you standing right beside me. What do ya say? *Marry me?*"

When she looked around, she saw glowing faces cover their mouths and point at their table in excitement. Raymond was what her mother had wanted for Jo all along. It was not just someone special, her mother had said so many times, but someone to be the missing piece to her puzzle. No matter how happy she was alone, an additional part of her would now be filled.

As Jo leaned over the table, she kissed him the hardest she ever had and said, "Yes!"

He placed a thin gold band lined with small glinting diamonds and a round emerald center on her finger. As she admired the stone, she smiled ear to ear and felt as if she was in an alternate reality where she'd received everything she had ever desired. He kissed Jo slowly and received applause from the rest of the restaurant. Both of their faces flushed red from the attention. As the claps died down and Raymond and Jo separated from one another, Raymond looked into Jo's eyes more seriously than he had all night.

"I know this is strange, but there is something I need to ask you before we go through with this."

Slightly startled, Jo was not able to get inside Raymond's mind and think of anything he would want to ask her in the middle of an engagement.

"Have you ever *hit* anyone?" he asked in complete sincerity.

Jo let out a wavering sigh and responded, "No, I haven't. Why would you ask me that?"

"I know you've never done something like that, obviously, but a while ago, I had a girlfriend, and it got to a point where she just became really violent. I don't really like to talk about it, but ever since then, that is just something I know I can't live with," he responded shakily. He looked from his cupped hands that rested on the sleek table to Jo's face.

Concerned, she said, "Don't worry. I would never do something like that."

Little did he know, the same had happened to Jo. She had been hit multiple times.

CHAPTER SEVENTEEN

———

Apollo was the talk of the town. Men wanted to be him, and women wanted to be with him. He became a Seattle golden gloves boxer at the ripe age of eighteen, and it felt surreal to Jo he actually wanted to be with her above anyone else.

He asked her out on their first date, the summer going into Jo's freshman year of college. After dating for a year and a half, he had been more gentle and caring than anyone would have ever known. He had two younger sisters and a single mother he appreciated wholly and was the man of every girl's dreams, from looks to personality. She was not quite in love with him, but she came close. Then, everything began to change after he had lost one of his biggest matches of the year. His looks were still the same, with a few added bumps and bruises, but his personality morphed from likable and gracious to someone who always found a reason to be upset. A new haze formed in his eyes, of rage and blame no one could seem to explain.

The biggest fight Jo and Apollo ever had was the beginning of the end of their relationship. It was about Apollo's constant hostility toward Jo regarding Johnny.

"Whenever I talk to you, you're always stuck at the hip with that Johnny guy!" He stood outside of Jo's dorm room and screamed through the open door. He drew the attention of the entire hall. They all stared at Jo with concern but also a crippling fear. "I just don't understand why your best friend is a guy. If you ask me, that is disrespectful to your *boyfriend*." He clenched his fists beside him as he worked himself up even more. Dark red rushed in his deeply pigmented skin, making his light brown eyes look even brighter from the stark contrast but just as angry.

Since Apollo was not in school and only saw Jo only on the weekends, he did not like that her best friend was a man, even though it was obvious that Johnny and Jo shared no romantic interest in one another.

"I don't know how many times I have to tell you there is absolutely *nothing* between Johnny and me," Jo responded, irritated. Her eyes traveled from Apollo to everyone who stared at her in the hallway. She lowered her voice to a calm tone in hopes it would relax him, but it did not. Clenching his fists even tighter than before, he grabbed Jo's arm and pulled her through the hallway, then down to his car. Jo resisted slightly, but once they had reached outside, she had given up hope of breaking free from his tense grasp.

As they sat in the car, he yelled outrageously. Jo stared at him from the passenger seat with blank confusion, genuinely baffled by why this had upset him in this way.

"You know what you could do to save our relationship?" he went on, and Jo thought it was the perfect time to roll her eyes but did not dare to do so. "You need to stop being friends with Johnny. I know you claim nothing is going on, but frankly, I don't trust either of you. So basically, it's either *him* or *me*?

The decision was not easy, and neither was being given an ultimatum. Jo had not wanted to choose between them, as they had served wildly different purposes in her life, but since it was clear she had no other option, a decision had to be made.

"Well, if you are going to make me choose, I'm not going to stop being friends with Johnny. So, I guess we need to break up then."

He looked at her with the scorching fire in his eyes he had every time he stepped into the boxing ring.

He spit out a sentence too quick to comprehend and opened his car door, and he walked around and opened Jo's, just to grab her arm and pull her out of the seat. He pushed her to the ground. She could not tell if it had been out of malicious intent or a simple mistake, and he was too proud to admit wrongdoing.

"I guess we're done then," he spat, then kicked dirt in Jo's face as he turned away and approached his car door. Jo kept her knees nestled deep into the soil, and her hands were cut from the scrapes of gravel off the side of the road. Apollo drove away, unbothered by what he had just left behind, and Jo stared at his car as it faded into the darkness.

———

The next morning, Jo was surprised by a knock on her door. Her roommate was still sound asleep, and she gargled air and silently blew it out. She opened the door and saw Apollo lean on the door frame as tears slid down his face, filled with pitiful regret.

"I'm so sorry, Jo," he said, and he sounded as if his crying would start up again at any moment. "Please forgive me. I don't know what came over me, really. You can be friends with Johnny. You know how jealous I get."

Eyes still foggy and knees throbbing from the bruises and scrapes she had received the night before, Jo spoke softly. "Apollo, what you did wasn't okay. We just need a break, alright? I think we both saw your true colors last night."

Although Jo had promised herself she was utterly done with Apollo. Although Jo had promised herself she was utterly done with Apollo, he looked helpless. He knocked on her door and begged for forgiveness so pitifully that Jo did not know what to think anymore. "Call me in a couple of days, okay? We can talk about it then. I really just need time," she said, with a slight smile to indicate she was no longer mad when in reality, she was unsure of what she felt.

A few days later, Apollo called Jo like he said he would, but he now approached their conversation with an expectation that Jo would take him back. He acted like everything was normal again as if his blowup had been a blip in Jo's imagination, and he no longer needed to feel sorry for his actions. To him, he had apologized, so it was over and done.

"Hey, Jo," he said in one of his brighter moods.

"Hey, Apollo," Jo was not nearly as happy as he. After a long pause, she began to embrace the awkward tension and she braced herself. "I thought a lot about what happened, and I appreciate you came to my school, but I think we need to call it quits. For now, at least." She tried to think of anything else she could say in an effort to soften the brutal blow.

"Fine," Apollo said. Jo was unable to read his mind and know what he thought, but she had an inkling it resided in the realm of fury. "I don't need you anyway!" he growled and quickly hung up the phone.

Letting out a breath of relief, she released every morsel of air inside of her, then hung the phone on the wall softly and returned to her day. She felt bad for what she had done to Apollo but simultaneously noticed a weight being lifted off of her shoulders, which she had never recognized was there, to begin with.

———

A week passed, and Jo had still not spoken with Apollo. Thankfully, Johnny made it known anytime she wanted to go out on a date, he would pluck the perfect man from his roster, but she was unsure what she should do with herself. She usually hated these matchmaking endeavors and did not know if it would benefit her to be alone or finally break and allow Johnny to run wild with his dating schemes. All she knew was she was lonely, and the sound of a date with one of Johnny's friends did not sound nearly as bad as it had.

Feeling slightly sad about the breakup and in need of a distraction, Jo said hesitantly, "You know what, Johnny? I could use a night out. If you really want to set me up on a date, I wouldn't mind."

"Are you serious?" Johnny responded excitedly, and his spine straightened immediately. Energy rushed through his body and caused him to ignite. "Great, I have just the guy. I will tell him to meet you at the Bellingham Bar on Friday. Say, nine o'clock?"

"Sure," Jo said with a chuckle, amused by just how elated Johnny was by something as small as this.

"Okay, great. You won't regret it, Joey!"

As she sat at the bar table, she wore more makeup than she had in months and a dress for the first time in a while as well.

She sipped a beer and was approached by an attractive man who wore a multicolored patterned sweater and baggy jeans. His beaten-up sneakers slid across the venue effortlessly, and he exuded a warm presence.

"Hi, are you Jo Sanders?" he asked politely, and as she nodded and gestured for him to take a seat. He looked at her kindly with his clear gray eyes. "I'm Philly Foster. My real name is Phillip, but everyone calls me Philly. Kind of weird, I know," he said with a scoff. His eyes scanned Jo, and she looked at him and was unable to identify his glance as endearing or odd.

Jo liked what she saw: a tall thin frame and shaggy dark hair. Jo was happy she decided to branch out, meet someone new, and begin her process of, if not entirely forgetting, getting over Apollo, who had taken over her life more than she realized.

She had a great time the entire date. They blew back drinks and successfully left the stage of simple small talk as they began to walk back to campus. They grew more comfortable around one another, and they held hands and laughed at jokes, which neither of them truly thought were remarkably clever. They walked farther into what now was darkness from the lack of streetlights. The stars shone brightly in the clear, darkened sky, and they heard a car rushing past quickly screech to a halt. A tall man crawled out of the car.

"What are you doing with my girl?" Apollo said with a shout, then came closer and stomped his feet against the pavement with a hardy force.

"Who is that?" Philly asked, then looked over at Jo anxiously in search of any explanation.

Apollo stomped toward them. There was a fire in his eyes once again, and his fists clenched tighter than ever before.

She looked at Philly with a dread that paralyzed her. She was unable to run or even walk away from the hurricane headed straight toward them.

"Apollo," she whispered. She squeezed Philly's hand a bit tighter and suffocated his fingers. Her thick rings dug into his skin.

"Isn't he that golden gloves boxer?" Philly said now and squinted to make out if he was right.

As Apollo approached, he paid no mind to Philly but held laser focus on Jo. He towered over her and quickly ripped out a fist, then punched Jo clear across the face. Her body crashed against the sidewalk, and she slammed her head against the pavement. Blood dripped down her forehead and melted into the grimy concrete. When she reopened her eyes and the light and shadow filtered back in, it was to the blurry sight of Philly as he ran away.

The outline of his thin body left Jo without a second thought, and Apollo stood over her and looked more terrified than she had ever seen. He stared at his hands, horrified at what he had just done, and he seemed unaware of his own power or the anger that resided inside of him. It certainly came out in the most evil ways.

CHAPTER EIGHTEEN

———

For the first time, Jo saw who Apollo truly was.

"I'm so sorry, Jo," he said with a wail. "I don't know what came over me. I'll never do that again, I promise." By the cracks in his voice and the uncertainty in his demeanor, it occurred to her she had never seen him like this: vulnerable.

He had always been known for his strength, his courage, his ability to break out of the norm and be a star beloved by all. But as she looked at him now sad, angry, and weak, he was no longer beloved by her. The very act of looking at him in this state made Jo nauseated, unable to hold in her anger and pain. She did not want to believe this was their new reality because he used to treat her with such kindness and grace. But now, everything shifted, and although she thought she could love him someday, that would never become a possibility. At this moment, he was simply accepted but never truly loved.

———

"Mom, I need you right now!" Apollo exclaimed in a crippling panic as he sat along the sidewalk and talked through the street telephone. The wire from the telephone stretched through the thin doors of the phone booth. "I did something bad, and you need to come and help me with Jo. Please, this is important!"

"No, Apollo don't," Jo replied, her voice stretched itself thin from the pain. One hand rested on top of her head, and the other supported her neck. "I don't want your help. I'll have someone else come. I don't need her to come, seriously."

"But, Jo, I want to help you! This was all my fault!" he shrieked, then walked toward her with both of his arms ready for an embrace, but Jo stepped backward quickly, disgusted by the thought of his touch.

"No, I'm okay, really." She responded calmly as she looked Apollo in the eyes. "I want to go home. I'll call you later, okay?"

Though Jo's college apartment was a few blocks away, and she had a small first aid kit at the ready, she wanted to go home, to her real home, back with her parents and brother who she desperately hoped would be there to let her in the door with open arms.

She knew she would be unable to track down Johnny, who she had never wanted to be in the presence of so fiercely until this moment, so she left. Apollo returned to his car and drove away per her demand to leave her be and shed a few rogue whimpers of regret. She walked across the street and found the nearest phone hoping she would have at least two quarters on hand. Luckily, after she scavenged through her purse and felt the pounding of her head, she found them. She cried on the phone like she never had before. The person she wanted to reach the most was Milo, and luckily, he had answered.

"Hello? Jo? Wait, what's wrong?" he asked, frightened by heavy breathing on the other end, as cries spilled out of her.

"Please, Milo. I really need you to come to my school and pick me up. Please come." Jo whispered desperately, and she begged for him to take her to the only place where she felt as safe as she needed to feel at this moment.

"Jo, I can't drive yet," he said, but his mind began to spin with possibility. "I could ask my buddy on the track team. I think he just got a car."

"Okay, I don't care," she said and blubbered. "Can you just come now?"

Crawling in the car, she turned her face toward the side window, so Milo wouldn't be able to see. He turned around and looked at her from the front seat, then stretched over and grabbed her cheek with the long bony fingers of a single hand. He shifted her face front to force Jo to stare back at him. Her right eye was swollen near shut, shaded in vibrant reds and blues. She was unable to see anything but vague shapes as though through a thick mist.

"What the hell happened to your face?" His voice was so loud her spine straightened almost immediately, and his friend snuck a look at her from the driver's seat. Jo did not respond, but Milo continued, "Jo, tell me what happened."

"Fine," she huffed and took a moment to collect her breath. "It was Apollo."

———

They pulled up to their home after few hours of open roads and brutal silence, and once they got out of the car, Milo's friend drove off. Jo released a sigh and indicated more than relief. She felt indescribable bliss. As they strolled to the kitchen, Jo trailed Milo as he reached his long arms into the freezer to dig for a bag of frozen anything to help with the swelling of her eye. It had now moved to its next stage and released mysterious secretions, and he chucked her a bag of lima beans, which made Jo shiver in disgust as she imagined the taste.

She rested on the couch for a while and sat beside Milo as he stared at an old magazine and pressed an icy bag on her eye and cheek. They were both exhausted. Jo glanced at the clock and noticed it was three in the morning, but she chose to stay up because she was now far too nervous to lay her head. She was too nervous to be on her own, even if the comfort of her old room and dreams were there to accompany her.

"You know Dad is going to freak out, right?" Milo faced toward her, then leaned to his right, so he got a better view of Jo's left eye.

"Where even are they?" Jo asked, relieved they would not have to see her in this state but already missing their presence.

"They went to Portland for the weekend for a 'quick getaway,' or however Ma described it. But they'll be here in the morning," Milo responded, worried for the future that stared them both in the face.

"Well," Jo said nervously. "I just hope he doesn't do anything too bad."

———

Jo had not been able to swirl into a slumber for more than three hours that night and awoke to the sound of her doorknob that ripped through drywall as her father busted through. He initially cracked the door to admire her unexpected company, but once he saw her swollen face, he became controlled by rage.

"What in the world happened to your face?" He stood in the door frame, and he paid no mind to the destruction he had just created. He marched up to Jo and grabbed her face. Her neck tilted up, and she looked at him as he towered over her and panted, furious.

Jo was not scared for herself but for Apollo. *What is he going to do to him?* She thought to herself. Whatever it was, it would not be good.

Racing down the stairs, barely awake, she felt her father's hand grip tightly around her bicep. Her eyes began to throb from regained consciousness, and they approached the kitchen to see Jo's mother.

"Oh my lord, Joey! What in the world happened to your face?" she yelped. Her mouth was frozen in the shape of an O.

As she leaned into her mother's chest, free from her father's tight hold, Jo felt comfort as her mother whispered delicate words into her ear. The light touch of her mother's hand smoothed up and down her back. It felt as though Jo stayed in her mother's arms for hours, but in reality, it had only been a few short minutes. Once they released one another, her mother wiped away Jo's tears filled with gunk, and her father was nowhere to be found.

"Sonny?" Jo's mother shouted in a panic. By the time she called his name three times with no response, they saw him. He marched down their street with nothing but his own determination and a sharp ax. "Sonny, what are you doing?" Jo's mother asked, stunned, and her high-pitched tone finally reached through the white noise.

"I know that son of a bitch boxer did this!" Sonny hollered back. "Not to my daughter. No way. He's not doing this shit to my kid." Sonny was ready for whatever the day would bring, on a mission for what seemed to be dressed as brutal annihilation.

CHAPTER NINETEEN

———

As Jo's father walked down the block, he swung his ax with plans to kill. Her mother dialed the police immediately. She desperately awaited an answer to her call as she watched Sonny from the window. He walked farther away and escaped her line of sight. The family saw the police arrive shortly after and stop him on the side of the road. He surrendered the ax after a short exchange, and they walked him home. The cops were unsure if this situation should be one of comedic relief to share with fellow officers or a frightening encounter that spiraled into a bloody homicide. Anger and thirst for revenge still filled Sonny. He stared at Jo as she iced her eye with a frozen chicken breast, which was the only thing her mother could find in the freezer because Milo had accidentally allowed the lima beans to thaw.

"Are you going to press charges?" her father asked bluntly after the police had gone and his hands clasped onto one another. His body folded within itself. Jo knew what he wanted her to say but was unsure if she was ready to grant his wish just yet.

"Honestly, I don't know," she responded hesitantly. She watched her father carefully for any indication of how he had felt about her answer, but his face displayed nothing.

———

After that punch, which happened so fast and felt almost surreal, Jo felt viciously affected by the memories. The fear and the anger she felt toward Apollo for his moment of weakness was disappointing, and she was ashamed of herself for how it altered her life so completely.

It began with a lack of appetite and sleep. Lying awake, she stared at her ceiling and checked the windows to ensure she was unseen in the dead of night. Fear consumed her in terms of what her father would do if he ever searched for Apollo again and what Apollo would do if he ever found her.

The longest Jo had ever gone without sleeping, due to the horrific incident with Apollo and the pain from her healing eye, was five days. She was barely able to walk. There was minimal energy left in her from the food she had eaten days prior. Although she had not eaten in a while, she never felt hungry, and she began to lose weight. Every time she ate, she felt a gargantuan pain in her chest and stomach. Her body rejected whatever it was given, even something as plain as mashed potatoes or white rice.

"You *have* to eat," her mother would say every day, and she would serve up big plates of food with sausage, potatoes, bread, and milk. She sat there across the kitchen counter and looked at Jo, who became frail and weak, and she forced her to swallow at least ten bites before she released her back to her room, where she would sleep for a great portion of the day.

Milo treated Jo as he normally would, and he picked on her sometimes and made jokes. Part of Jo believed he knew she would be fine. *Maybe this is a phase? She needs time to heal.* He had faith in Jo and her strength, she thought, and he knew she would overcome this situation.

Her parents did not feel the same and worried more than she ever thought possible. They checked on her every morning and night to make sure she was alright, and they worried she would rather starve herself to death or worse.

"Are you going to file charges or not?" her father would ask multiple times in a day.

Eventually, Jo responded, "No, I'm not. Apollo is a good man, and he doesn't deserve that."

Sonny stood up and walked around the kitchen table, where the whole family sat in the morning. He leaned down and grabbed both of Jo's arms to shake her out of this haze. The disappointment was overwhelming.

"Well, I'm not going to force you to do anything." Sonny began, and he continued to hold Jo's upper arms. "But that's a damn shame, and frankly, I'm disappointed." He did not even finish his meal like he did every morning. He just walked out of the house and headed to work.

For a month, Jo was sleep-deprived, and she felt pressured to eat, which caused a constant flow of anxiety. Jo had felt certain from his actions his punch was the final goodbye. Then, Apollo had reached out to her. Milo and Jo were the only ones home on this particular afternoon, as their parents went fishing for the day. As they lay on the couch and discussed mutual complaints about their parents and all of Milo's future plans, the phone rang.

"It's probably Ma or Dad," Milo said as he lay on the sofa and stared at the hacky sack his friend had recently given him. He flopped it up in the air and waited for it to plop back onto his chest. "Jo, can you get it?"

As Jo got up from the floor, she wiped the flecks of dust and fuzz off her corduroy bottoms. Then, she walked to the kitchen and released the phone from the wall, and she twirled the soft yellow wire through her fingers.

"Hello?"

"Jo? It's Apollo. I'm so sorry. Please come back," he said quickly, worried she would hang up at the initial sound of his voice.

Milo could tell who it was by the sight of her fearful eyes and the color drained from her face. Apollo had said something else to Jo before she had the chance to escape his call, and even after she hung up the phone, his last words lingered. Immediately, Milo walked over, snatched the phone from her hands, and pressed it against its wall hook. The sound of its ding was so loud it pierced both of their ears.

"Don't talk to him," Milo said sternly, and he pointed his finger in Jo's face, which he only did when he was serious. Unable to speak, Jo was horrified by what Apollo had just spit through the phone before Milo had saved her.

"Jo?" Milo said, and he slightly bent down. He looked at her face, stuck in the expression of panic. "What did he say?" he asked, now worried.

Jo was unsure if she should tell Milo or what she should do, but she looked at him. She tried to hide the horror in her face. "He said he's going to kill himself," Jo said shakily. Her eyes were frozen open. They turned glassy, and they welled with tears.

Milo reached his arms around her for comfort.

Her father walked through the door with a fishing rod in hand, just as Jo started to cry. It was like she could never tell what he would do next.

Her mother, who trailed behind at first, quickly moved to stand in front of Jo. "What's wrong?" Jo's mother asked as she tried to clear her throat and wipe away the remnants of tears.

"It's Apollo... I'm not sure if he's being serious or not, but..." Milo paused, then scanned around the house for any distraction. He hoped he would not look into his father's or Jo's eyes by mistake. "He said he's going to kill himself because Jo left him."

After they heard this, it was apparent their father was concerned, not for Apollo, but for Jo. "You know, Joey..." he began. He set his fishing supplies on the ground and leaned against the wall. "In this world, we're not responsible for anyone's life but our own. What Apollo does is his decision to make, and something which you can never blame yourself for."

That was all he said as he wiped under Jo's eyes with his cracked fingers. He cleaned them of their salty residue and went to prepare for dinner. Her mother trailed behind him, and she looked worried, but she did not want to cloud Sonny's message. He was right. There was nothing she could do, and so she did nothing.

Jo no longer answered the phone when it rang, and she continued to feel bad for leaving Apollo but knew they must remain apart. Jo did not know what Apollo would do, but no matter how worried she became, it would always remain out of her hands.

CHAPTER TWENTY

——

The next morning, after Jo and Raymond's engagement dinner, Jo showed her mother the ring on her finger, spotless, shining in all its glory. The only other time her mother had looked this happy was when Milo was born. She had been barely six years old at the time and was unable to recall much, but in retrospect, the only image Jo could vividly see was how happy her father and mother were. They had birthed the boy Sonny had secretly wanted for so long, and fulfilling this wish had made her mother happy. Although Sonny loved Jo as much as any birth father would, when he held Milo for the first time, he knew he was *his* straight from the beginning. It was a moment none of them would ever forget.

Planning a wedding was something Jo had not thought much about, but she quickly realized the immensity of the work and time involved.

"First, we have to book a church. I believe Raymond's parents have an idea of where it should be," her mother rambled on as she sat beside Jo on their dining table and spread out the notes she had made for Jo's wedding. "Next, flowers! I love dogwoods, so maybe we should have those. What do you think?"

Her mother moved from an upright seated position to a full stance, and she waved her arms and paced around the kitchen as she continued her speech.

"I'm not a huge fan of dogwoods, Ma. What about peonies? Those are *my* favorite," Jo responded, and she crossed her arms and remained seated.

As Jo was able to see the thoughts that spun through her mother's mind, Emi sat back down and returned the papers she had picked up during the conversation of wedding details. She turned toward Jo and leaned forward slightly, and she grabbed both of Jo's strong hands with her thin ones.

"You know, Joey," she said, as she moved in closer, and she changed her energetic aura of celebration to one of delicacy. "I'm sorry if I'm being a bit much. I just want you to have the wedding of your dreams, with all your family there watching you. We are so proud of how far you have come." That was all her mother had dreamed of on her own wedding days, and both times, those prayers went unanswered. Her family was not there to watch her. They were disinterested in the person she had become.

———

After weeks passed, as they stood in front of a congregation of faces, some of which Jo recognized and some of which she did not, she felt endless support for her and Raymond's relationship. She was nervous, and she shook and breathed shallowly as she looked into Raymond's face. His lips quivered in anxiety, and his body buzzed with the swirling of excitement and anticipation. She knew he was the man she was meant to marry, and they were both riddled with pure excitement.

They both said, "I do," and the crowd screamed with combinations of applause and tears of joy. Jo turned to face her mother. She looked at her eyes, which blared a bright shamrock green and reflected the bright church lights. Tears had not yet fallen, but they were building. Jo rarely saw her mother cry and could not recall ever seeing tears from her father in her lifetime, but the two of them looked at their daughter with admiration and disbelief as they both tried to reel in their emotions. They failed greatly. After all this time, her mother had gotten the wedding she had dreamed of. In truth, it was not for her. It was for Jo, but judging from her reaction, that had been enough.

As people sat around packed tables topped with bouquets of bright peonies and subtle dogwoods, Raymond and Jo sat at the head table with their hands intertwined. Jo watched her mother and father dance in the center of the floor, and they shined in their love for one another.

"Do you want to go dance?" Raymond asked softly as he saw Jo's eyes well up with tears. "Your parents are adorable. I don't think I have ever seen two people love each other that much." He squeezed Jo's hand a bit tighter and felt the hard points of her wedding ring. "Besides us, of course." He chuckled.

"Yeah, they're great," Jo responded, and she patted under her eyes before tears could disturb her neatly done makeup. "Sure, let's go dance."

As Raymond and Jo rose from their table and walked up to Jo's mother and father, both couples smiled at one another, and the two of them danced in unison. They slowly rocked back and forth to the harmony of "(I Love You) For Sentimental Reasons," and Raymond's fingers tightened around her waist. The side of his ear pressed against hers, and her father looked at them lovingly. As she looked into Sonny's eyes, which were a usual dark midnight, surrounded by a vivid white, tears now filled them.

"I love you," Sonny whispered to Jo. The bottom of his face tucked in Emi's done up curls.

"I love you too," Jo responded with a slight smile and returned to look into the eyes of her future.

As the song came to an end and a momentary quiet filled the air, Jo released Raymond and strolled around the room. She smiled at all who'd attended. As she walked closer to the exit and made rounds, she stopped in her tracks when she saw Elaf stand by the walkway.

"Jo," he said, relieved as they made eye contact. He quickly walked up to her and grabbed both of her upper arms lightly. "You look absolutely stunning."

"What are you doing here?" she asked, concerned. His face had changed more drastically than she imagined it would in this last year. His skin now resembled the texture of a walnut, with its premature dips and wrinkles.

"One of my buddies heard you were getting married, and I just wanted to see it for myself. Who would have thought?" he began sarcastically. "Jo actually had the guts to go out and marry someone else when she knew how much I loved her. I'm not going to lie. I feel a bit betrayed… disappointed, really."

As Elaf continued, Jo was in utter disbelief. "You should know you are too good for this dipshit you are marrying, and my door is still open if you want to ditch this place right now and come with me."

She felt as though she was in some sort of fever dream or nightmare.

"Elaf, I really don't know what your problem is with me... I really don't. We broke up, and now I'm happy and *married*, and you made the decision to get divorced, okay? I really understand you are in a tough place, but if you are here to stir up some drama, all because you are disappointed your life isn't working out as you hoped, then you need to go." Jo pressed her hands against Elaf's chest and made an effort to nudge him toward the exit. As she moved him two steps back, Elaf lost his balance. He wiped Jo's hands away from his body and pushed her to the side.

"Elaf, stop!" Jo said as he walked toward the dance floor, then looked around for the man who had stolen Jo away from him.

"So, who's the groom?" he shouted, and he halted the music and everyone's conversation simultaneously. As the silence became stronger, Raymond remained seated. He looked around for Jo and resisted eye contact. "Well, whoever you are, you're a coward. I hope you do whatever you can to keep Jo because if it weren't for you, she would be marrying *me* right now and not your sorry ass."

As Jo walked up to meet him on the dance floor, she hoped Raymond would not identify himself, and she looked at her parents as they held each other in their confusion.

"Elaf, you need to go *right now*," Jo said sternly, and she grabbed his arm and dragged him out of the venue. Everyone's eyes were glued on them, and a smirk was plastered on Elaf's face. As they arrived at the exit, everyone's heads turned toward them, and Jo's eye makeup had already smudged from the chaos.

Elaf looked down and grinned at Jo, pleased with himself and the destruction he had caused. "Well, my work here is done. Hope you have a great rest of your reception." He slammed the door closed and left Jo in front of it.

She turned to face the crowd. "I am so sorry, everyone. That was just a huge misunderstanding, but everything is fine now. Everyone go get some more food and drinks, and let's keep this reception going!" she said, and attempted to lighten everyone's mood, which included her own.

Jo slithered through the crowd, and she held her gaze downward until she had finally reached her table with Raymond. He looked up at Jo as she found her place and sat next to him.

"Who the hell was *that*?" he asked quietly, and he waited to raise his voice as the music turned back on and the two of them sighed in relief. Jo looked at every point in the room except for his direction. Once she had finally met his eyes, she sighed and began to cry silently.

"That was the last boyfriend I had before you," she began reluctantly, and she leaned her hands forward to touch Raymond's. He accepted them with hesitation. "We broke up when I went to New York, and he was really upset about it. I guess he still isn't over it." Her voice began to waver. "I had no idea he was going to do that or that he even knew about the wedding. I'm so sorry." As Jo cried harder, the music drowned out the sound of her whimpers.

Raymond cupped her hands tighter and leaned in, and he pressed his forehead against hers.

"Hey," he whispered, and he showed his bright teeth in a slight smile. "It's okay. I wish you would have told me so that shit-show didn't just happen at our *wedding*," he said, and they both giggled. The color resurfaced in Jo's face. "We'll be okay, and for all we know, this could be a really good story in a couple of months."

As he released the pressure of his forehead from hers, they both sat up, and Jo patted her tears away with a dinner napkin.

"Okay, well... you handled that so much better than I thought you would," she said with a slight chuckle. "I love you," she exhaled, and she turned her head toward him. Raymond did the same.

"I love you too... but you already know that."

CHAPTER TWENTY-ONE

Five years later…

It started one night a year into their marriage. Raymond laid beside Jo as usual, and his eyes grew heavy from fatigue. Then, he posed a simple question. "When do you think we should have kids?"

From the time they'd started to date, up to their wedding day, they had both expressed their desire to have children of their own and made small comments here and there. They'd planned names, how many they wanted, and when they wanted to have them. Through multiple conversations about both their work and the *right time*, they decided they wanted at least one year of marriage with no children or pregnancies, and they had done just that. But after that year had passed, and they began to put efforts toward getting pregnant, luck did not come their way. Jo's womb struggled with the ability to hold a child. Hope deteriorated, and worry rose between them. They were unsure why Jo was unable to get pregnant.

Jo and Raymond visited many doctors, and even though Raymond was a physician himself, he did not know what was wrong. The best advice they had been given was, "Just keep trying. Nothing appears to be wrong, so keep your fingers crossed, and your dreams might just come true." The doctor's face looked chipper with his painted grin. She resented his happiness and inability to give straight answers.

Nothing appears to be wrong, so keep your fingers crossed, and your dreams might just come true. But that was easier said than done. Jo, Raymond, and the doctor all knew that to be true.

———

Jo woke up especially early one morning and went to the bathroom. Then, she felt a turning in her stomach. It ached so badly she felt turned around and threw up.

Before Jo had come up for air and continued with her grunts and releases, Raymond was awake. He leaned beside her and held her stomach lightly, and he pulled her hair firmly over her ears and behind her neck to allow space to breathe in between releases of vomit.

"Maybe it is what I think it is," he said and immediately went to the living room, grabbing his keys off of the counter. He said, "Wait there. I'll be back in ten minutes!"

When he returned, with his wrinkled brown bag and keys in hand, he stood over Jo, who rested on the bathroom floor. Her pain had begun to subside, and her ability to stand came back once again.

"What did you get?" Jo croaked, and she rubbed her stomach with the tips of her fingers.

As he reached into the bag, he pulled out two pregnancy tests and smiled at her. He quickly tried to erase the smile from his face, as he did not want to get Jo's hopes up or his own.

"You are showing symptoms, so we can just check," he said nonchalantly, and he switched to his professional voice, which displayed his doctorly demeanor.

As Jo pulled herself up, she leaned on the bathroom sink and Raymond's arm simultaneously. He handed her a pregnancy test.

"I'll be back in a few minutes," he said and grinned, and he let her know he was excited for this reveal of their future, but also, if it was not what he had hoped for, then everything would still be alright. There would be no reason to feel sad or disappointed because that was an emotion they had felt countless times before.

Sitting in the bathroom, alone, pajama shorts around her ankles, and a pregnancy test below her hips, Jo did what she had to do and set the test on the sink. It rested in preparation for its reveal, which held the potential of changing both of their lives forever. As two minutes soared by, Raymond knocked lightly on the door he would not to startle her.

"Have you looked at it?" he asked, and he cracked the door open and revealed a sliver of his face. His childish excitement beamed through the door frame.

Staring down, her eyes grew wider and breath shorter. Raymond walked in completely and held up the moist stick.

"Oh, shit," he said in near disbelief. "We're pregnant!" He was glowing as if he was pregnant instead of Jo. He looked at her face as they stared at this test with two thick pink lines, and they both began to act bubbly with all-consuming joy.

CHAPTER TWENTY-TWO

———

Giving birth to their daughter was a moment Raymond and Jo never thought would truly appear. Jo lay in the nursery and held her tight, and she glowed with the light of the sun, which shone through the pink and yellow linen curtains.

Raymond sat beside her. He gazed upon his daughter and considered her something more special than any miracle. When sitting close to Jo, he looked at both girls in his life with unfathomable gratitude. All he said was their daughter's name, and he touched her small doughy hands and grazed his fingers against her skin.

"Willa," he muttered calmly, and he looked up at Jo's face to receive any indication if she liked the name. "It means protection, and I know as long as we are alive, we will protect her. Forever."

They had not discussed a name during Jo's pregnancy because neither wanted to get their hopes up.

"How about this?" Jo had said one late night as she lay beside Raymond on the bed and rubbed her full belly as she felt sporadic kicks. They were prepared for their daughter to arrive any day now, and Jo had grown tired of the back pain and fatigue. "Once we see her, once we hold her in our arms, one of us will know the name, and that will be it."

Now, they'd found one. It was a name more perfect than either of them had ever imagined. She was their Willa, and they would protect her with everything they had. Forever.

———

When Jo walked into her childhood home, she saw Milo seated on the couch with his arm around his girlfriend, Penny. She was a young woman with gorgeous brown eyes, which were bigger than the moon and shining just as bright. Her mother and father stood beside them and anxiously awaited their grandchild. They did not yet know her but already loved her unconditionally. Raymond held an over-sized diaper bag and the rest of their belongings as he opened the door for both Jo and Willa.

Emi nearly cried as she saw the baby nestled in her own daughter's arms. "Oh my goodness, me," she said, and her voice wavered from uncontrollable emotion.

Jo walked closer to her, and Willa drifted in and out of sleep. She fidgeted from position to position. Jo transferred her from her own arms to those of her mother, and when she held her, tears filled her bright eyes. She was so touched and overwhelmed she could not help but cry.

"She is just the most beautiful thing I've ever seen," Emi said, and she looked into Willa's round eyes and at her silky dark hair, which was already long enough to form loose curls.

As Jo's father walked up to the three of them and lightly touched Willa's hand, Willa smiled and leaned in toward him. He took Willa from Emi and wrapped her in his arms.

These were the arms that used to wrap Jo and let her know she was safe, and he would protect her, and now, her daughter.

––––––

As Raymond, Willa, and Jo stayed with Emi and Sonny for the next few days, her mother could not stay away from Willa. She held her and showed absolute love with every chance she had. Jo loved to watch her mother and baby girl interact. She watched from the living room as Emi held onto Willa tightly in the kitchen and explained to her the ingredients she added to a new maple pecan pie recipe. She spoke to her in a squeaky voice one uses when they speak to a dog. It didn't matter to her. There was no chance Willa would understand a word she said. They already loved each other even in those first days. Emi loved Willa the way she loved Jo, if not even more so.

"So, Milo…" Jo began, with the entire family scrunched at the dining table and everyone broken into pairs. "Not to be too forward or anything, but what are your and Penny's plans for the future? Are you thinking about getting married?"

"We aren't really sure yet," Milo answered and looked at Penny. The two of them clasped hands. "Just living in the moment," he explained.

Once Milo answered, and the conversation began to lose life, the energy in the room seemed peculiar. It was not as laid back or relaxed as it had been every time they sat and ate at this table. The problem did not lie with Milo, or Penny, or even Jo and Raymond, but their mother and father. They said very little. The only noise that came from their direction was Willa's little hiccups, and sporadic mouth pops as her grandmother bounced her about on her knee.

Sonny sat beside Emi, and he held her hand and looked in his wife's direction more times than usual. He did not glance but looked with purpose. He checked to see if she was eating her food, paid attention to everyone's conversation, and looked around.

As Jo sat next to him on the sofa later that night, she bounced Willa on the edge of her knee and watched television with the rest of her attention. Meanwhile, Sonny continued to look over at Emi in the kitchen.

"Dad?" Jo asked quietly, so her mother would not hear them over the television that played in the background. She had drawn his attention away from her mother for possibly the first time that evening. He turned to Jo as she looked down and smiled at Willa endearingly.

"What is it, Joey?" he asked.

As she looked into his face, she tried to give him the message he needed to pay attention to her. This was serious. She whispered, "Is something wrong? I mean with Ma? You look a little stressed out."

Jo waited for an answer. Her father realized he was too obvious, so he attempted to appear more aloof. He quickly slouched a little deeper into the sofa and interacted playfully with Willa.

"I don't know what you're talking about. I'm just admiring my wife," he said casually, but Jo could tell by the overenthusiastic expression on his face and how his voice rose an octave that something was amiss. He either was unsure of why he did this, or he did not feel the need or want to tell Jo.

"Okay," Jo said reluctantly. "But if something is going on, you'll tell me, right?"

All he did was nod and return to the television. He tried to grin at Willa but could not help but look at his wife once again. Distress was scribbled all over his face.

PART THREE:

WILLA

CHAPTER TWENTY-THREE

———

Willa could tell by the way Dawson looked at her something was off.

This was not the usual loving gaze he threw in her direction whenever he made a charming remark or apologized for something he had done. Rather, he had a look of unease. Before he stepped foot into her home, Dawson looked at Willa and mumbled under his breath, "I think we should break up."

He made panicked eye contact with her, with his hooded eyes centered in thin gold frames. Willa had built a world around the role models they were to other couples in their high school for the past year, and now that had ceased to exist.

Dawson Jenson was the type of name you read in the yearbook, and before you saw the picture, you knew he was gorgeous. The tale of their relationship was unpredictable to most but seemed plausible to Willa. She'd had feelings for Dawson since she entered high school but knew it was far-fetched because it did not seem like Dawson even knew her first name.

When Willa walked into school the first day of junior year, there was a shift in her demeanor. She started at this particular school sophomore year because she had told her parents reluctantly she would stay in a religious all-girls school throughout high school. But after she attended that for middle school and her freshman year, Willa knew this could not go on, and she begged her parents to let her transfer. It came to the point she would much rather gouge her eyes out with dull communion crackers than sit between two nuns at the next mass.

With this newfound confidence and comfort she had in this newer, co-ed school, she noticed people treated her a bit differently. Although Willa maintained a strong friendship with her old friend group, she received invites to more parties and get-togethers as well. This was how she caught Dawson's eye, and somehow, something happened between them.

It all started with the Halloween party that was the talk of the eleventh and twelfth grades for all of October. The year before, it would have been ridiculous to think she would be invited, but this year was a different story. Seated in the library alone after school, she scarfed down sweet potato fries drenched in ketchup. Willa watched one of her new favorite films, *10 Things I Hate About You*, on the library television.

Constance, the known host of all the best parties of the year, casually walked up to Willa's lonely table and sat down. "Hey, Willa. What are you doing for Halloween?"

Willa swallowed the last chunk of sweet potato. "I don't know yet. What are you doing?" Constance quickly plopped down a small, printed flyer and slid it in her direction. "You can come if you want. Most of our grade and the senior class is going to be there."

As Willa read the poster, which beamed with neon colors and photos of all things Halloween, she looked back up into Constance's annoyingly perfect porcelain face and nodded. "Okay, thanks. Maybe I'll see you there."

———

For this event, Willa dressed up as Donna Summer, a disco legend she had been obsessed with since she was little. However, none of her peers seemed to know who she was except for some of their parents. They complimented her costume and told her fond stories about their childhood disco experiences in the 1970s as they dropped their children off and gave a final goodbye.

As Willa danced with her friends and twirled alongside them in their poorly made costumes, she laid eyes on Dawson. He was dressed as Marty McFly from *Back to the Future*, which was also a costume no one seemed to recognize except for herself. When she gazed at his dirty white sneakers, up to his neatly placed sandy hair, Willa let out a gasp that vacuumed all the air from her surroundings into her stomach.

He noticed her as well. He saw she was somewhat buzzed, which was why Willa started to wave at him with no shame, but he smiled. He moved his hand up to give a slight "hello" back and smiled brightly. At that moment, Willa felt the urge to grab her necklace tight and choke herself into oblivion. She was convinced it had been a pity wave. Looking at him in embarrassment and shock, Willa waved again childishly and quickly shuffled to the bathroom to collect herself.

When she finally emerged from her hideout, she stuck by her friends' sides and avoided eye contact with Dawson. She remained glued to her group, and she cringed as she relived what happened, in that horrifying moment she hoped she would forget by morning.

Constance held the unwavering opinion it was essential to have a Halloween party on the actual day, which fell on a Thursday. This meant Willa went to school the next day with a slight hangover, in addition to the cloud of embarrassment hung over her head. Although her friends told her it was nothing, she felt otherwise. No matter how little these moments felt to others, for Willa, she always managed to trap them inside of her mind and overthink into an oblivion.

Later that day, as she sat at the lunch table with her closest friends, Willa noticed that Dawson had sat down at the end of the table. This time, she did not gasp or wave awkwardly, but she felt a pit in her stomach and was convinced this was torture. She repeatedly looked at Dawson and swiftly jolted away before he noticed. Willa got up to get another serving of food and felt someone lurk behind her.

As she waited in line, she was surrounded by people who talked and laughed, but she did not have anyone to converse with. Then Willa felt a tap on her shoulder. When she turned around, she looked up at Dawson, who towered above her.

Her eyes turned into saucers, and blood swarmed to the apples of her cheeks.

"Hey," he said with his silky tone.

"Hi. What's up?"

"My sister and I are going to a concert this weekend, and I know you're kinda friends with her, so I was wondering if you wanted to come? We have an extra ticket, and she brought you up."

She looked at him as the wheels turned in her head, then muttered, "That sounds fun. Can you text me the details?"

"Sure thing," He nodded. "I'll get your phone number from my sister then." He walked into the distance, and Willa did everything in her power not to break out in celebration.

———

As she arrived at the concert in her embarrassingly bright red Ford Taurus, Willa looked around for Dawson to let him know she had arrived. After a few brief minutes, she noticed he wore an outfit of cropped jeans and a cuffed old t-shirt.

"My sister and her friend are waiting in line, and we're pretty close to the front," he said with a grin.

"Okay, cool. I just have to pay for parking."

As Willa walked over to the meter and Dawson followed, she was forced to pay twenty dollars for the evening. She noticed the machine only accepted cards and had made the unfortunate decision to only lug two wrinkled twenty-dollar bills in her shallow overall pocket. Dawson glanced at her anxiousness and reached into his wallet to nudge his credit card in Willa's direction.

"Here. Don't worry about it," he said kindly.

Walking into the venue, Willa was greeted by Dawson's younger sister and her friend, who accompanied her. They both carried womanly assets that were unbelievable for someone who had just entered ninth grade, and the two were eager for the night ahead.

"Hey, Willa. How are you doing?" his sister Aster asked in a tone deep that was raspier than Willa had known it to be. "I feel like I haven't seen you in so long. Excited for practice to start up again?"

"I'm good," she responded and made full eye contact with her, so she did not have to look at Dawson for too long. "And yeah, it'll be fun having you on the high school volleyball team this year."

The concert was fun and freeing. Willa had mainly stayed glued to the sides of Dawson's sister and her friend for comfort, but the moments she had alone with Dawson felt unreal. His personality was much sweeter than she had envisioned. She began to see him as an actual human being rather than the perfect character Willa had built in her head.

As they left the venue, to Willa's surprise, she had made a moment of flirtatious eye contact with a boy who stood outside of the concert doors. She had never seen this boy before, but he looked at her as though he were about to come up and make his move at any point in time. Willa looked at him and then looked away a few times. This flustered behavior had once solely been dedicated to Dawson, but now things had changed. Aster nudged Willa's shoulder.

"You should go get his number or something. He's totally checking you out."

Willa turned toward her, panicked. She looked up at Dawson, who seemed slightly disappointed. This was a reaction that struck her as confusing but slightly exciting. Before Willa could reply, Aster strolled over to this mystery man. They chatted for a moment, and when she returned, she held a handwritten phone number on a ripped receipt.

"Here. You're welcome." As she pranced to Dawson's car, one arm intertwined with her friend's, both Willa and Dawson looked at each other intensely.

That next week at school, she sporadically conversed with the boy she had made flirtatious eye contact with at the concert. It seemed to be all Willa's friends, and Dawson's sister could talk about.

"You know what you should do?" Willa's friend proposed. "We should talk about him in front of Dawson and see what his reaction is. You said he looked kind of disappointed when you got this guy's number, right?"

"I'm really not sure if that's a good idea," Willa replied. Her friends were dedicated to fueling drama, and they involved themselves in everyone's business. They would find out one way or another.

Seated at their usual lunch table, Dawson sat down to talk with his friends at the end of the bench. Willa's friends practically shrieked with the thrill.

"This is our moment," whispered one friend who sprawled across the table. Based on her glee, she believed she was quiet, but to everyone else, she screamed, "Look at me!" with her volume and drastic movements.

As Willa looked at her, she made it clear she was unamused. She gave her a stern face, which she only brought out when she was seriously unhappy. She continued, "So Willa, have you been talking to that guy from the concert? He was *really* cute, right?"

Dawson quickly turned his head in their direction, and shortly after, collected himself to put up a front he was unbothered. Willa looked down at her fingers and twirled her thick silver rings around her knuckles in discomfort. She went through the motions of what seemed like a pointless performance, but as she left the lunch table and began walking to class, Dawson's voice trailed behind.

"Willa! Willa! Can I talk to you for a second?"

Turning around, baffled Dawson had run after her, she responded, "Yeah, what's up?"

He pulled her to the side of the hallway to avoid passing students. Willa waited, and then, he tossed out a question, which she had only imagined, but never envisioned as reality.

"Do you maybe want to go out sometime?"

Willa froze for a few moments, and she looked deep into his dazzling eyes and smiled. "Sure."

CHAPTER TWENTY-FOUR

———

After Willa and Dawson's first date, which was a simple stroll around a vast park shadowed by budding spring trees, not only did their relationship escalate romantically, but they continued to see each other almost daily. Through dates and continuous interaction, they had become the best friends either of them ever had.

For over a year, Willa attended all of Dawson's family events. She constantly received invitations to their packed Friday night dinners and any minor holidays, such as the Fourth of July, or his father's big fiftieth birthday party, where the whole Woodson family made an appearance.

Out of everyone in Willa's family, it surprised both her and her mother that her father had taken such a liking to Dawson, as he was the first boy Willa dated. He had to face the fact Willa was no longer just a daughter and child but an independent woman with a love interest. Willa's father and Dawson discussed music, sports, and so on as they sat and watched whatever sports game was active in that season. Dawson's favorite sport was baseball, and so was Willa's father's, and they bonded over that.

"Willa, I like that boyfriend of yours," her father said randomly one night as he sat at the dining table to share a family meal. "What are you guys going to do for college? Stay together, I hope."

Willa cringed. She had thought about college ever since she entered senior year, but she was not ready to face it head-on. She found herself unsure of what she planned to do and was unaware of Dawson's wishes for the future of their relationship.

They rested together on a park bench, and both read and listened to the lean runners fly by, and birds chirp sweet songs in the distance. The two were silent for what felt like hours. As they read books they exchanged, they avoided an inevitable conversation as the school year came to an end and college decisions were announced.

"We should talk about what we are going to do when we graduate," Dawson whispered as he placed his finger in his book and slid the other hand against its broken spine. "What do you want to do?"

As Willa turned, she inhaled a deep breath and placed her finger inside of her book as well. She was slightly disappointed that she had to stop at such an exciting scene but realized it would not have been the appropriate time to ask him to wait.

"I've been thinking a lot about it," Willa began and started to reminisce on the good times they had shared, and even worse, her father's reaction to what she would say. "I think we should probably break up. We're going to be across the country, and I don't think it is going to work, but we should still be together until the end of the summer." As she finished her statement, she began to feel her throat swell and tingle. Dawson shifted his glasses slightly to wipe a developing tear.

"I agree," he said, and his eyes shined vivid blue and began to turn bloodshot. Both of them returned to their stories, flipped through pages, and watched people pass by. The strangers admired this young couple that read books together, which seemed to be a rarity nowadays.

They did not discuss how they would move and leave each other until Dawson stood at her door that day. He did not wait until the end of the summer as they had agreed. He did it only a week after their conversation. He was ready to call it quits, and at the time, Willa felt betrayed.

———

It was a relationship consumed by memories that stuck in Willa's mind, no matter how desperately she wanted to forget. Though they had dated for over a year and were inseparable, the connection was bound to come to an end.

Given Willa's move to California to pursue the life of a documentarian and Dawson's plan to live in New York, it was inevitable. Although she'd chosen for them to be ripped apart, the fact he had done the deed so shortly after their discussion made it even harder to bounce back.

She left for school a few weeks after they decided to part, excited for the change of pace. She felt it was necessary in order to move on from Dawson, who had been her entire world.

As she barged the door open, with an obscene number of boxes in hand, Willa was met by someone she would come to know as Rory Moore.

"Hey, what's up?" Rory quickly said with an abnormally large smile. Her teeth practically gleamed, and this expression allowed her concave dimples to stand out more than they would have otherwise. Before Willa could take a step farther, Rory dropped what she was doing to help. She grabbed a box from Willa's own hands and took it to Willa's bed without a word or expectation of gratitude.

Willa felt like she was hit by a truck. Rory's presence and charisma held the ability to stuff a room. As quiet and introverted as Willa was, it would have baffled her and Rory to learn they would become such close friends.

Surrounded by freshmen drenched in anxiety, Willa felt ready to start anew and obtain unfamiliar experiences along the way. She began to make friends fairly easily and no longer worried about fitting in or finding people she could sit with in the cafeteria. She was more worried about what she would gain from college and if she would make the right decisions for her future. She also wondered if she could rearrange her path to somehow accommodate Dawson in the future. Even though Willa had not made this clear to him, she hoped something would change.

As Willa overanalyzed what she would gain from her new journey, she knew college remained the window of opportunity where people felt free to make stupid decisions. This was a four-year ticket to find yourself, and Willa was ready.

Willa wanted to make sure she would have classic experiences. At the same time, she was somewhat held back by the fear of losing focus on why she was in school in the first place. Her brain ached with nerves every morning and night. She wondered if she made the right decisions, studied the right things, and thought about Dawson regularly, and wondered if they were meant for each other or if the past was a distraction.

"Rory, what do you want to do after you graduate?" Willa queried one night as she watched various dance shows the on small desk television, despite her own inability to dance.

"I'm not really sure. Just trying to figure it out, I guess. My parents didn't go to college, so me coming here, doing nothing, and then eventually graduating with a degree in anything is impressive to them," she responded casually. Their eyes were still glued to the screen, and their bodies twitched to the static beats of the music without intention.

"What do *you* want to do?" she asked. Rory was one of the only people she had ever known who did not compare herself to others. That was one of the biggest things Willa appreciated about her.

"I want to be a documentarian, but I just hope it works out," Willa said. She noticed Rory no longer paid any mind to the conversation. Her eyes were still glued to the screen. Willa's fingers twirled over one another, and she felt a buzzing in her temples.

"That's pretty cool. Probably cooler than what I'll be doing." Rory said and did not show any sign of discomfort or self-doubt. She knew whatever she would do would be great for her, and what others did didn't concern her, even though at times Willa believed it did.

Rory noticed Willa's distress did not ease up, even a few days after their conversation, so she felt compelled to step in. She figured some forced socializing would remove Willa's insecurities.

As she stormed into their dorm room one day, when homework was the only thing on Willa's mind, Rory once again commanded the stage.

"You know where we should go?" she said with a smug look and deep enthusiasm. "I'm taking you to a party tonight, and before you say anything, it's going to be the best time of your life. You're going, and I don't want to hear any of your shit," she said and made an effort to look intimidatingly sober but already failed desperately. The night had barely even begun, and Rory had already left two empty boxes of wine on her desktop.

As Willa looked up from math homework, she gave Rory a small grin and began to giggle with excitement at her upcoming journey in the hopes of the college experience she needed.

"Fine, I'll go." Willa knew there was no other choice but was secretly excited about it.

For Willa, whose high school graduating class was a measly fifty students, this party felt like another world, and Rory ate up every second of it. As they choked down shots of lemon vodka and played beer pong with an intensity as if lives depended on it, Willa felt relaxed for the first time since she entered college. She did not even think of Dawson. Surrounded by new faces, one boy caught both Willa and Rory's attention immediately. His looks were striking, and they learned his name from a girl who noticed the mystery man gazing. As he conversed with the crowd of freshman girls who swarmed around him, it was evident he was admired by many.

"He's cute, huh?" a random girl asked casually and stumbled into Willa. She was a drunk mess.

"Yeah, who is he?" Rory responded immediately, unintimidated.

"That's Raimy Kita. Every girl is in love with him because he's a poet or something, but he seems like he's either really hard to get or a total ass." She slurred and went through her monologue as if she had given every freshman girl the very same rundown. "One of you should definitely shoot your shot, though. You never know what might happen and you are hot enough. Seriously."

As she stumbled away, she gave Willa and Rory a sloppy hug. Rory looked at Willa up and down as if she had proclaimed her the chosen one, who was destined to have her shot with Raimy Kita. She knew she would be unable to escape this task as long as Rory had something to do with it.

The next day, as Rory and Willa saw him stroll through campus, they admired him from afar, and he became one of their daily conversation starters. He was what everyone wanted out of a college boy: creative, well-dressed, and social.

A few weeks into school, Willa and Rory realized they needed to party less and become involved in more beneficial campus events. They decided it was in their best interest to involve themselves in a club they could do together. One afternoon, in between classes, they looked at their options. Willa sat on her bed and looked over Rory's shoulder as she flipped through the school catalog.

Rory quickly came to a halt and looked at her with thrill. "Yes! Environmental club! This is what we need."

"What? Why the *environmental* club?" Willa said, confused by Rory's sudden interest.

"All hot guys care about the environment, and that's a fact," Rory explained, and Willa rolled her eyes. As she thought about Rory's point, she realized she might actually be right.

On the first day after discovering their passion for the environment, they walked into the club room and were astonished by its members. Although Rory had made it clear there would be an attractive bunch of people who would protest climate change worldwide, they had no idea just how astonishingly beautiful they would be. The girls and boys were abnormally attractive. They strolled around in their vibrant muumuus and overalls and seemed to show genuine interest in the subject matter.

After they had managed to find a seat amongst the group, they were stunned by the turnout, and they watched as the president of the club walked in. Of course, it was Raimy Kita. He wore a plum-colored t-shirt that read, *The Earth is a fine place and worth fighting for* across his chest. The words of Ernest Hemingway.

"Hi, everyone. Welcome to the start of the year! My name is Raimy, and I'm the head of the environmental club and go-to person for any questions or ideas you might have to make this space the most beneficial for ourselves and Mother Earth."

He stood proudly in front of his clan, and he stated he was a junior who studied business and environmental ethics and minored in women's studies. He hoped to run his own nonprofit organization. It was evident he enthralled everyone in his presence, and now so was Willa.

"Okay, this is better than I thought," Rory whispered. The intensity of her smile and change in body language revealed her thoughts. "Now you totally have an in. If you don't get with Raimy by the end of this semester, I will be highly disappointed in you," she said jokingly, but she and Willa both knew it was not really a joke.

CHAPTER TWENTY-FIVE

The environmental club's meeting on limiting plastic use on campus wrapped up as each person secretly realized the school would never agree to their propositions. Rory persistently nudged Willa toward Raimy as bodies began to file out of the room. Rory acted as if she had gone back in time and was now in the third grade. She put forth her best effort to embarrass Willa to no end, and she succeeded.

"Stop!" Willa hissed as she tried to resist and slide the sleek soles of her shoes on the squeaky floor. Rory pushed her struggling body.

Eventually, Rory pulled her hands off of her and whispered, "Bitch, if you don't get the balls to ask Raimy out right now, I won't let you drink my alcohol before the next party."

Willa looked at Rory and sighed deeply, rolling her eyes. Willa stomped over to Raimy and watched as he conversed with a freshman girl who looked as if she wanted to pounce on him. She showed absolutely no concern for those around her.

"Hey, sorry," Willa said and interrupted their conversation. The girl glared at Willa with beady eyes. Though she tried to act unbothered on the surface, it was clear to Willa she was out for blood. "Raimy, can I talk to you?" Willa asked, and he immediately turned toward her.

He blocked the other girl's view of his face with his broad shoulders. All his attention was on Willa. "Absolutely. What's up?"

Willa plotted the question in her mind but felt too afraid to ask. She looked at Rory, who peeked around the corner, though she pretended to have left the room long ago. She lurked in the shadows as she waited for Willa to take the plunge.

———

To Willa and Rory's disbelief, Willa discovered a burning passion for the environment. Apparently, it had been buried deep inside her until now. After she participated in this club for three months and was asked to take a leadership role in their advocacy, she found a new part of life she would enjoy. Besides Rory, Willa's second closest friend was now Raimy. She was still romantically intrigued by him but believed they would remain friends.

Their friendship began in earlier meetings when Willa was still intimidated by the fellow planet lovers, but they had both come out of their shells, and their friendship held its own. Although Willa intended to ask Raimy out as Rory had planned, she could not build up the courage since she'd made the painful decision to friendzone herself. She and Rory hung out with Raimy at times and chatted with him after meetings, but in her eyes, the ship of romance had sailed.

As Rory and Willa walked around before meetings, they talked to other fellow first-years. Willa hid behind Rory in an attempt to blend in the background of the conversation.

Willa let Rory do most of the talking when Raimy came up to the group and hesitantly tapped Willa's shoulder.

"Hey. How are you?" he asked with a slight smirk. His lips were a deep oak color, and his skin was a lively copper.

As she turned and saw it was him, Rory noticed her chance to support Willa's involvement with this desired man and immediately led her new acquaintances to the other side of the classroom. She paid attention to her own conversation while listening to Willa and Raimy on the opposite side of the room.

"I'm good. How are you?" Willa asked, confused, unaware of why he had only sparked this conversation with her.

"I'm great. I've noticed your involvement in the club has been really amazing, and I just wanted to say I'm really excited to have you in a leadership role. If you ever want to hang out or talk about club stuff or anything, I would be down anytime," he said, and he looked sincere as he always did.

"Thanks, I'll remember that."

"Well, great. I'll give you my number, and we can definitely get coffee or something." As he reached into his back pocket and pulled out a pen, he gestured for Willa to free her hand. Willa placed her open palm in front of him and watched as he wrote his number on her skin. He smiled, then released her grasp.

"Alright, well, I'll see ya," he said and walked away slowly.

Willa had never gotten coffee with Raimy, but with his number on hand, she felt a newfound confidence. Rory cheered on the endeavor as usual. She and Raimy talked regularly, and it appeared more plausible their new friendship could escalate to something further.

"Now, since I clearly don't have a chance against you, you should ask Raimy out. You being his friend is a waste of time, and you text him nonstop anyway. You might as well take the plunge." Rory explained in the dark. The two girls were tight under their covers, and Willa was ready to sleep.

"Do you really want to be giving him high fives at parties after he makes out with people that aren't you? That would be a friendzone you could never escape from. Tragic, really."

"No way! He likes me as a friend, and I don't want to embarrass myself." They went back and forth until they no longer had the energy to continue. In the end, Willa reluctantly buckled and agreed she would take a chance and ask Raimy out the next day.

"You know what, fine. If I do it, can you finally go to bed?" Willa said. Rory zipped her lips tight for the remainder of the night. She quickly dozed into unconsciousness.

Willa's heart pounded, and she felt a jolting pinch in her ribcage. Nerves tickled her limbs and made her feel as if she swam in a pool of rice. She already regretted what had not yet been done and began to sink in anguish.

———

"Hey, this is super random, but I was wondering if you wanted to hang out sometime." Willa watched Rory from the corner of her eye. She jumped up and down as she peeked from behind the wall. Willa felt her heart pump harder and harder.

The cramped classroom spun as Raimy grinned and muttered in a hushed tone, "I'm down," and nothing more.

Willa felt as if she had not quite understood the meaning of Raimy's simple phrase. It had been much more underwhelming than anticipated.

When Willa walked away, Rory was bursting at the seams.

"See, I knew he would say yes!"

"Was that a yes?" Willa asked with genuine concern.

Rory jumped up and down, obviously sure it had been. The two walked out the door with a pep in their step and made their way back to their room. Rory eagerly waited to hear every detail, even though she had just seen the event with her own eyes.

"I know this is more of a casual date, but you still need to look good," Rory said as she helped Willa apply her makeup.

Willa hated the way it felt on her skin. It clogged pores and turned her face into a rubbery prosthetic. But today, she would have to deal.

Willa was nervous for this date, not only because it was with Raimy, who seemed to be on the entire student body's wish list, but aside from Dawson, she had never thought of anyone else romantically. This was an opportunity to stop thinking about the relationship behind her and venture on this date with someone who had sparked her interest. Hopefully, this would be something as great, if not better, than the relationship she once knew. Maybe the memory of Dawson would become hazy.

"Okay, you look amazing. I'll release you," Rory said as she finally let go of Willa's face. She finished her last application of a berry-colored blush. It reminded Willa of blood oranges or rich summer plums and smelled like an artificial rose. As Rory grabbed Willa's bag, she gestured her out of the room, and she freed a caged bird to live her life and then come back and tell her all about it.

As Willa walked to the door, nervousness controlled her. She could already feel her legs shake, and instant regret took over her stomach. It churned with remorse and embarrassment for the awkwardness she was certain would ensue.

"Good luck!" Rory yelped. "I can't wait to hear all about it!"

Seated on a couch covered in salt and vinegar chip remnants and the hefty odor of cigarettes, Willa and Raimy watched *Fight Club* on a small television screen. This was not quite what Willa imagined as a *first date*, but now there was nothing she could do to change it. Their legs glued against one another from the humidity as they sat and watched the painfully bright screen. Willa was unsure what kind of relationship she wanted with him.

As the movie progressed and the tension grew, he placed his hand on her thigh, and panic ensued in her. Willa had not known Raimy in this way even an hour ago and felt it was not the right time. As she sat on crumbs, amidst the filth and odor of a filthy early twenties male apartment, she made her decision. Although this date was as good as any she supposed, Willa wanted nothing more.

But before she had time to answer his touch, Raimy's tongue slipped into her mouth and made its way swirled and nearly reached her clenched throat. Shivers rushed down her crooked spine and into her toes. He tasted of marijuana and desperation, and his hand began to trail quickly and reach for body parts as if he did not know where anything was.

As she heard the sounds of bodies banged against chilled concrete and blood that splattered from Brad Pitt's doing in the background, with puffs and coughs in the corner, Willa knew she did not want to go any further. She had genuinely wanted to make an effort to get to know him apart from what he was able to do in the bedroom. Even though this had just begun, she was already tired of going through the motions.

"Hey, can you stop for a second?" she asked, unaware of what she was supposed to do to end an unwanted advance. She slid her lips away from him, then pulled back with force, but made an effort to appear nonchalant to avoid discomfort.

Raimy released his grasp and looked at her, puzzled and profoundly offended by what Willa had just done. "What's wrong?" he asked with flecks of judgment in his tone. He had already grown upset by the slight pushback.

"Nothing," she responded. There was an uncomfortable pause as she was unsure what to say next. "I just thought the point of this date was to get to know you more… like talk."

He scoffed as if he had to explain to her what this situation was. "You asked to *hang out*, not *go out*, so I thought you just wanted to hook up." As he said this, Willa received the message loud and clear.

She cut him off and sighed tiredly, "I'm not really in the mood, and I would have rather gone on a *real* date, like outside of your apartment, but that's fine. If you change your mind, let me know, but otherwise, I'll see you at our club meetings or something."

As she stood from the dented couch, she brushed the salt and vinegar residue off of her legs, feeling the burning sensation from the worn leather. Raimy remained seated.

"Okay, I'll let you know."

She waved at him sarcastically and turned to leave his apartment. As she did, she saw his roommates smoke from a bong in the corner of her eye, as they had been for the length of her stay. They laughed about one of the new freshman girls they had made a bet on.

College boys. You can't live with them, and you *can't live with them.*

CHAPTER TWENTY-SIX

———

Weeks passed, and all Willa heard in the stuffy classroom were Rory's remarks. She made fun of a situation Willa still did not find funny at all, but she hoped she would eventually.

"It's so awkward we still have to come here," Rory said. "Is it weird seeing him after what happened? I would totally be embarrassed," she continued with a slight chuckle.

"Yeah, but it's fine, I guess," Willa responded nonchalantly as she saw Raimy at the head of the classroom. He droned on about eliminating plastic water bottles on campus, and his voice began to muddle through Willa's ears.

Meanwhile, Willa began to relive the atrocity of the date. Despite her discomfort, Rory continued.

"He keeps looking at you. Eww, I am so disgusted. Can he not?" Rory whispered every time Raimy shifted his head in their direction. He would pretend he had a crick in his neck or wanted to look around the room as he stared at Willa. As Raimy continued his *unintentional* glances, Rory could not let it go. Willa did not want to be the hot topic to cure Rory's boredom. She just wanted to forget it ever happened.

After this situation, Willa found thoughts of Dawson continued to randomly creep in her train of thought. She knew she should not think about having any type of relationship at all, but instead, focus on herself, which was something she had not remembered since the early years of high school. It was time to move on. She did not want to think about Dawson or any possible relationship or romantic arrangement. The time had come for Willa to come to her senses and put boys on the back burner.

Just when Willa believed things had reached a turning point, Raimy approached her in the middle of campus. She sat alone on a creaky wooden bench in the middle of the school garden. New buds emerged, and different flowers sprayed their sweet scents into the air as she listened to the calming sounds of birds chirping. Willa finished up a homework assignment before she headed to class.

"Hey, whatcha doing?" he asked calmly. He slightly gestured with his right hand she should look up from her laptop. "I thought about what you said after we hung out a couple of weeks back, and I wanted to know if you wanted to go out with me sometime? Like on a *real* date."

She clicked her laptop closed and slowly straightened the slope of her neck. Willa squinted. She looked at his smug face, entirely perplexed by the situation.

"It's been three weeks," she said dully, with an undertone of angry sarcasm. "Why do you want to go on a date with me now?"

Given the circumstance, Willa believed this to be an entirely fair question, and after a tedious back and forth, he had somehow convinced her to hear him out.

"I keep seeing you at meetings and realizing I messed up. You're pretty cool, and I want to get to know you more." Raimy seemed nervous, and he rocked back and forth on the heels of his worn Vans sneakers.

Willa was still glued to the bench as he looked down at her. Her bare limbs became sticky from sweat and humidity in the air.

"Okay, fine." She looked up at Raimy, who now perked up. He no longer swayed back and forth but stood with the strength he usually emanated in their group meetings. "I'll go out with you."

As Willa told Rory every detail of the event that had just transpired back on campus, Rory was beside herself.

"I can't believe you are going out with him again." Rory began, unsure of how upset she should be. She sat beside Willa on her bed and shook her head softly, and she laughed at the ridiculousness of Willa's decisions as if she had not done something nearly as bad before. On this day, Willa ranted with Rory about how she needed an official break from boys, then agreed to go on a date with the very subject who made her want to cut herself off in the first place.

It was embarrassing but something Willa had to deal with. Her decision had been made, and there was no other option than to follow through. Part of her was truly curious to see if he had changed his ways.

———

As Willa sat across from Raimy on a small circular table at the local diner, she watched as he inhaled handfuls of French fries dipped in mustard and slurped a vanilla shake. This date had been going better than Willa imagined, but it was not a time she would hold dear to her heart for years to come either.

"So, how was your day?" She tried desperately to make small talk in an attempt to break some of the buzzing awkwardness.

"It's been good," he replied. As they spiraled into a further conversation about his classes and what he wanted to do before he graduated, it brought ease to Willa's mind not to have to carry the conversation. She was actually interested in some things he had to say. Eventually, they ran out of topics to fill the silence with, and it became obvious they both felt uncomfortable. They listened to the laughing of other college students in the background who spent time in groups of friends or on dates as well.

"So, after this, do you want to see a movie?" Raimy asked shyly.

"Sure, that sounds fun." Willa eagerly waited for him to finish his meal. He led her out of the door and walked with a sense of urgency that caught Willa off guard.

They walked for a while, and they managed to pull a few topics out of thin air, from the Southern California weather to upcoming class assignments. Raimy came to a halt and gestured to his apartment complex, which Willa had not noticed they were near until their arrival. She looked toward the door and already smelled the stench of weed and cigarettes. The empty bags of candy and potato chips that littered the lobby floor disgusted her.

"Okay, after you," he said as he gestured to the door with an obnoxious smile.

"I thought we were going out to see a movie?" Willa said, confused and beginning to close herself off. She stepped back from Raimy slightly.

"Well, movies are expensive, so I just thought we could watch one in my room again. And my roommates aren't home this time, so we'll be alone. Better, right?"

Willa felt put on the spot. At the same time, she felt unable to turn his proposition down. She entered the building and made her way to his apartment. His place brought ultimate disgust to those who breathed in its nauseating stench as they walked to the entryway. Willa sucked in her last clean breath.

They rested on the same couch, which never managed to rid itself of the salt and vinegar chip crumbs that scraped at the bottoms of Willa's thighs. Now, they decided not to watch a movie, which Willa preferred, but a show, at Raimy's request. They watched *South Park,* a program Willa hated with a steaming passion, which managed to enthrall every boy between the ages of ten and twenty-five with its outrageous and problematic humor.

The episode continued with the paper figures on the computer screen, which hopped from side to side with their squeaky voices. Raimy began to shift closer to Willa. He made an attempt to feel her touch, and she knew what would happen.

Willa received a sense of clarity. Not only had their conversation throughout the night been not particularly interesting, but she felt they had nothing in common besides the environmental club and being Black in a mostly white school. It was clear now she was not very attracted to him, and the more he introduced comments and bragged about his family and his many accomplishments, the more repulsive he became to her.

She remained beside him with her arms crossed along her stomach. They squished her belly to brace for further displeasure, as Willa was not in the mood for what he plotted. He turned toward her and waited until she looked at him, then breathed a bit louder now to draw attention to himself.

Once she did, Raimy quickly grabbed Willa with both hands. He gripped the sides of her neck and violently stuck his tongue into her mouth, then swished it way back down her throat and cut her airway. For a moment, Willa felt lost. Then she rediscovered herself in a state of shock. She was unable to move, unable to advocate for herself, and felt as if she was in a dream state. She almost felt this was not real.

As she managed to regain power over her body and pull away from him for a brief gasp of air, Willa spit out, "Stop. What are you doing?" Her voice squeaked, and his spit trickled down her chin. She rubbed her hand against it, and a shiver rushed through her arms.

Raimy only responded with a direction to hush and pushed her to get on top of her. He used all his weight and force to pin Willa down and began to make an effort to rip off her clothes with a single hand. As she came out of the daze, where she had felt too startled to move, she pushed him off with every bit of strength she had, then dug her nails into his chest.

"I don't want to do this right now!" she exclaimed as she panted for air and glared at him as if he had just committed the worst of crimes.

"*Right now?* Does that mean in like five minutes, you'll stop giving me mixed signals?"

Willa pushed him in disbelief. She sat up as fast as she could from the worn leather seat and made her way to the door, as he said, "If you didn't want to hook up with me, we shouldn't have gone out on a date. This was a waste of my time."

More than feeling disappointed in Raimy for his actions, she felt disappointed in herself for going against her previous wishes. It was a trend for her to only succumb to men who only cared about their best interests. It was clear Raimy could not care less about her.

Willa managed to walk herself home in the chill air, still in a state of disbelief. The rubber of her boots squeaked against the cement, and she was unwilling to make eye contact with the men who passed by her as the sun set. She slouched on her bed immediately after her return, and Rory sat next to her. She stroked the crown of Willa's head as she cried and offered Willa the remnant of a joint, even though she knew full well it was more than a week old.

"Here, this will take the edge off. I know it's kind of grimy, but it will still get the job done," Rory said in complete seriousness. Her voice sounded somber.

Then they discussed how often boys were not what they seemed to be. Raimy was a beloved person in their school and especially in the environmental club. He was even known to advocate for women's rights, as women's studies was a minor of his in school, but now that struck the two as a complete joke.

"I'm so surprised he would do that. What a dick." Rory exhaled smoke into their already muggy dorm room. She continued to brush Willa's head, and some of her fingers intertwined with her thick brown curls. "You just never know what kind of person you're dealing with until you're put in a situation you might not be able to get out of. I'm just sorry that happened to you, Willa."

When Willa opened her eyes the next morning, she saw Rory fast asleep in her own bed, directly across from her own. She still wore the jeans and sweatshirt she had on last night, and Willa felt her eyes caked with the crust of dried tears. As she sat up and walked over to the sink, she stared at herself in the mirror. She looked down at the gash which had been torn on the side of her once favorite top. She had not noticed it until then.

"You should get him to pay for that, you know," Rory said groggily as she began to regain consciousness. She stared at the shirt as its rip began to fray. As Willa turned toward her blankly, she looked back at her own reflection and stretched the side of the shirt to look at its irreparable gash. That was the *least* he could do.

CHAPTER
TWENTY-SEVEN

Ever since Willa's incident with Raimy, club meetings and her passion for environmental advocacy hadn't been the same. Willa dreaded going to meetings with every fiber in her being. When she saw Raimy, he looked at her with embarrassment and blame. She felt as if her stomach spun in a turmoil of eternal nervousness.

As she saw him day in and day out, she promised herself and Rory she would not talk to him again.

"You have nothing to say to him, *right*?" Rory asked her before their first meeting since the encounter. "If you say anything, tell him he owes you money for your ripped shirt. If you start talking more, he may try and weasel his way back in, and that's the last thing you want." Willa looked up at Rory and chuckled. She thought about how ridiculous it seemed, but Rory maintained eye contact and held her arms sternly.

"Willa, *seriously*. What he did to you isn't okay, and if anything, he owes you that much. After you get your money, you never even have to say another word to the guy."

Willa thought this over as they walked into the war zone with their arms intertwined. Willa knew she was right. He did owe her.

After Rory and Willa attended meetings for a week, and perfected the art of selective hearing, Rory left early to meet friends for a group project, and Willa was on her own for the first time. Given Rory had all her belongings in hand, it was clear she would not be back, and now Willa was left feeling isolated, uncomfortable, and alone. As soon as Rory walked out of the door without looking back, Raimy stared at Willa with intent. He knew she could see him, but he did not care in the slightest. It felt like he wanted her to see.

He held an unwavering gaze in her direction for the entirety of the meeting, and Willa did everything in her power to resist eye contact, so she would not give him any form of satisfaction. Once the discussion ended, she was prepared to grab her things and run out of the door. When Willa reached down and snatched the thin strap of her backpack, she felt someone behind her. She felt his eyes inspect her from her head to her toes.

"Hey, can we talk?" Raimy said. Willa could sense through his inflections he had rehearsed that question many times before. She turned around slowly and saw Raimy look at her with what once was a charming grin. He took a step forward. "Please, Willa. Can we talk?"

Willa nodded once and felt immediate regret. She began to play out the lecture she would receive from Rory that night as Raimy began a spiel about how he was sorry Willa was uncomfortable on their date, but ultimately, he felt it was not his fault.

He went on for minutes that passed by as slow as molasses. As he spoke about nothing substantial, Willa lost the ability to hear anything he said.

"Are you going to pay for my shirt?" she interrupted. "You ripped it that night, and it was important to me."

She spoke this phrase as more of a statement rather than a query, and Raimy immediately gave her a smug look. Now, she had become used to its constant appearance.

"I'm not paying for your shirt," he scoffed, unable to tell if that was a joke. "It's not my fault I ripped it, and it's not my problem you're upset about it. I'm sure you have the money."

The snap in his voice made Willa aware he had morphed into the dark Raimy she had witnessed that unforgettable night.

She rolled her eyes. "This absolutely is your fault, but if you're going to make a big deal out of paying for it, then don't bother. Just don't talk to me anymore," she said bluntly. She was tired of his refusal to hold himself accountable for his actions.

As she stomped back to her room, with no money for the ripped shirt, Willa realized the blatant disrespect. This incident made the memory of Dawson's break up with her seem like an act of an angel. Willa did not know if it was her, college, or just boys in general, but it seemed as though no matter who she met or how different they were from one another, they all made her feel like everything was her fault. *It's not my fault I ripped it, and it's not my problem you're upset.* This rang in Willa's ears as she neared her room, and tears formed in her eyes. Her cheeks scorched red hot through her sun-kissed skin. She knew it was not her fault. She knew Raimy was simply a selfish person, but she still felt bad for her actions. She wondered if there was anything she could have done to have prevented that mistake, but she was unsure what she could have done differently.

CHAPTER
TWENTY-EIGHT

After Willa found clarity about the kind of person Raimy was, she was now on a journey to find closure and acceptance. She considered it the final straw in her causal romantic endeavors. Although Rory had some unpleasant experiences herself, she was still hopeful and searching for *Mr. Right*.

Rory was an expert in dating sites, but Willa was far less experienced. While Willa was entirely too skeptical of the possible risks, Rory had been on dating sites since high school, and she even managed to lose her virginity to one of her lucky matches when she was sixteen.

"When I got there, he was shorter than me, which was awful, but he was still cute, so I went for it anyway," she explained the first time she told Willa this story. After they knew each other for only a week, Rory already felt comfortable enough to tell her about several sexual experiences. Rory wanted to make Willa a dating site covert but also understood Willa needed a break. She insisted once Willa was ready again, she should try it out.

A few weeks into Willa's new life of independence and abstinence, Rory told her she had planned a date for this weekend with a boy she had met on the newer site, eHarmony. He was someone who fit her ideal type almost too perfectly. He was the tallest Korean man she had ever seen, armed with a muscular sleeve of tattoos and earrings. For Rory, it seemed like the opportunity of a lifetime.

"Willa, you don't understand," she began as she stared at her computer screen. She showed her a smoldering photo of the very subject. "He is literally my dream, and he's in our town. That doesn't happen."

Rory rose for the next day, more excited than she had been about anything. She wore her usual leggings and a cropped sweatshirt to show just enough skin.

"Wish me luck!" she said as she skipped toward the exit. "Let's hope I don't get abducted."

As Willa watched Rory drift away, excited and fearless, Willa wished she could be more like her. She wanted to have no fear, to be spontaneous, and not to care about what anyone said. As the door slammed shut behind Rory, Willa stood still and hoped this date would live up to Rory's great expectations. She walked back to their room and sat on her bed. She watched a movie and finished her homework for the weekend, and she eagerly anticipated the call she would get from Rory to tell her every detail.

———

Willa buried her head deep within a mountain of pillows, and she heard nothing but the quiet screams of an awful 1970s horror movie. She began to drool on her notebook scribbled with numbers and letters of math problems she would never comprehend. Willa began to doze, then jolted awake when her phone rang.

Willa lifted her head slowly and answered the call. All she could hear were loud cries and slurred words. They came out in distressed shrieks.

"Rory, what's wrong?" she asked, now fully awake. She pressed the phone to her ear with as much force as she could.

"It was awful!" Rory hiccupped. She tried to catch her breath. Willa heard the ambient noise of the rain tapping against a windowpane. She worried about whether Rory would drive home with care. "I can't talk about it right now, but I'm never doing that again. Can you be awake when I get home?"

Willa looked at the clock and saw it was now two in the morning, but of course, she agreed to wait. She wanted to hear every horrific detail of Rory's date with a man she had been so confident in just hours ago. Although she knew it had gone badly, she still hoped for some good news or even a funny experience to make the event worth it. When Rory came home, she ran into the room and hurled herself at Willa. She pressed her head into Willa's body with a heap of force.

"What happened?" Willa asked as Rory released from her grasp momentarily and looked her in the eye. Her makeup was splotchy from her tears. Barely able to talk or even breathe, she pushed words out of the pit in her stomach. She gasped and let out the most tragic cry Willa had ever heard.

"He... He..." she began, and Willa thought Rory might never finish her sentence. "He... *raped* me, Willa." Rory cried even harder. She did not believe a girl such as Rory, with so much confidence and strength, could be taken advantage of in this way, but she was proven wrong.

CHAPTER TWENTY-NINE

—

As days passed, Rory and Willa were silent. Willa wanted to bring up what happened to Rory, but there was never a right time. *When do you ask someone what exactly happened when they were raped… and how?* She concluded you did not unless they bring it up themselves first, or they fall down a hole of pain and isolation so deep they cannot crawl out of it alone.

As Willa held her tight that night, at five in the morning, she still heard the cracks and sniffles of Rory's soft cries but said nothing. She only broke the silence once when she no longer heard Rory make any sound but was sure she was not asleep.

"I'm here for you. If you need anything, just let me know, okay?" Willa tried her hardest to stay awake but was barely able to keep her eyes open. She did the best she could to be there for Rory in a time where she did not know what else could be done. She was unaware if her presence had made any difference in Rory's agony at all. She hoped it did.

After Willa spoke, Rory didn't do anything. She didn't even murmur the softest of sounds to indicate she had understood the comment just spoken. All she did for the rest of that long and terrible span of darkness was lay still. Her eyes were barely open, and Willa didn't know what she was thinking. She felt unable to speak. Rory no longer had enough water left inside of her fragile body to cry. Her eyes were glossy, and they mimicked the look of a fresh corpse as spheres of unmistakable horror.

When Rory began to open up again, she no longer talked continuously or kept up with the latest dramas as she did before. She loosened the reins on her clenched demeanor ever so slightly, though. Willa sat next to her in bed as she did homework a few nights after her crying spree. She looked at Rory plainly until Rory stared back.

"I know you probably don't want to talk about it with me, but I think you should talk to someone," Willa said.

Rory's expression changed from neutral to misery. "That's not gonna happen. I'm fine. And besides, you didn't talk to anyone about that whole Raimy thing, and you're fine, right?" Rory responded. There was a bit of annoyance in her voice.

"No, I didn't, but at least I talked to *you*. I told you everything, and you won't tell me a single thing. We're supposed to be friends, and now you're just shutting me out of something that I can help you with."

"You just won't understand, Willa! It's not about you and what you want or don't want to hear. Just let it be about *me* and what *I* need, please. This is so much worse than that whole train-wreck with Raimy, and you know it. Unlike you, I actually have a legitimate reason to be upset while you whine over a boy who won't even reimburse you for a stupid ripped shirt."

Willa knew her night with Raimy was not as bad as what Rory had gone through. Rory had been in a realm of violation beyond her. This feeling of helplessness and shame would creep in her deepest nightmares and trail through the lingering thoughts of her past, possibly for the rest of her life. Raimy was a questionable person, one who needed to reevaluate his morals and treatment of women. However, Rory's situation felt far more worrisome, but Willa did not want to admit it. Rory's inability to share the details pulled them apart. As best friends, they should be inseparable in times like these.

"I know I don't know what you went through, and I didn't tell anyone about Raimy. Looking back, I wish I did, but now I feel like it's too late. You still have time, Rory. This is serious. And if you ever want to tell someone, you can always tell me. I wish you would, just so I can help you more."

Rory nodded and turned away. Rory was unsure of where to look or what to do, so she looked everywhere but in Willa's direction.

"I'm done with guys," Rory huffed as she moved to lay on her stomach. Her eyes were now stuck to the square display of light that rested on her bed, and she typed rapidly.

"You can say that shit again," Willa agreed immediately. "And besides, summer is just a week away. Pretty soon, we'll both be back home and have three months to reset and not think about guys at all."

She had not realized summer was so close until she said it aloud. Willa was excited to return to Washington and do exactly what she told Rory she would do. She wanted to reset and forget about the bad events of this year. Summer would be a time of relaxation, no drama, and especially no boys.

CHAPTER THIRTY

———

As Willa heard the wheels of the plane abruptly land with a skid upon arrival to Washington state, she had never felt more relieved to be in a place she had often taken for granted. Her home, which she was ready to escape from just months ago, was now a destination she needed more than ever. She was eager to see her family and return to a space that once was her world.

As she walked through the airport with an oversized duffle bag and suitcase in hand, Willa pushed through the doors and escaped to the outside. She smelled the familiar scent of wet concrete and fog that drifted in the soft breeze. Then she saw her mother's face. She stood just outside of her car and smiled ear to ear, as if she had not seen her daughter in years.

"My Willie!" she said as she opened her arms for a fervent embrace. Willa hated when her mother called her that, but since she had not seen her in a few months, she let it slide.

"Hi, Mom," Willa said quietly, as she accepted her hug and felt comfort from the scratch of her mother's rings as they rubbed up and down her back.

"How was school before you left? Any cute *boys* I should know about?" By the way she said this, Willa knew her mother secretly hoped she had gotten over Dawson. Willa's mom liked Dawson fine, but she was worried for Willa and what her father would do if she circled back. Since she and Dawson broke up, her mother had seen the brutal reality of just how much of a mess Willa truly was. She often cried, for little to no reason at all, and when her father stayed late for work and was unable to see her ridiculous sleeping habits, Willa would lay in bed for the entire day and cry. Her mother had only come in to check if she was still breathing and to leave food on the bedside table in hopes her appetite would improve.

"Are you okay, honey?" she always asked but knew the answer. Although Willa was nowhere near the realm of *okay*, her mother continued to ask. It was clear she hoped there would be a day when her daughter would hurt less, and she felt confident that day was near.

As Willa barely answered the questions her mother asked, she put her belongings in the car and sat in the passenger seat. As they drove past the towering trees and delicate scents of floral and pollen, they spoke casually about classes and Willa's excitement for summer. But ever since she had asked her about Dawson, Willa had been thinking of him. She thought of his soft hair, calming voice, and the way he'd broken up with her so quickly. He had abandoned her before she could give a substantial goodbye, and ever since, she could not stop thinking about him. *How is he? What is he doing? Is he home for the summer?*

————

As Willa lugged her suitcase through the door, with her mother trailing behind, they both walked through the hallway. Willa left slight traces of dirt on the cherry hardwood floor and saw her dad standing in the kitchen. He did not carry his usual serious demeanor. Joy transformed his face. His pure jubilation was evidence he had missed her after all this time.

"Hi, Willa. How was your flight?" he asked casually and walked over to give her a light hug. He helped her with her suitcase. Willa's father was not a man to show much affection, but there were small hints.

As they sat around the table, they silently ate a homemade dinner of eggplant parmesan. They picked at their slightly overcooked dish until Willa's mother said something to spark conversation.

"Raymond, how was work today?" she asked.

Raymond responded with elation, as he loved to talk about his work and lectured about how many births he had delivered that day and the exciting drama that had ensued. As Willa listened to him go on and on, first engaged but now fading away, she thought about Dawson, no matter how hard she tried to resist. *Is he home for the summer?* She wanted to know but would not put forth an effort to find out.

———

After just a few days of living at home, Willa felt like she had never left. Once she finally finished her overdue packing, her old routine took shape like she had never gone to college at all. She sat on the pilling carpet of her bedroom floor and flipped through the pages of her journal. She pulled from the abyss of her disorganized backpack. Willa grabbed a pen from the inside of the front cover and turned to the newest fresh page. She struggled when she thought about what to say, considering how much had happened since the last time she had summarized her life in this way.

With a random spark of inspiration, Willa wrote about Rory and Raimy, but after a few sentences that covered both of these topics from her recent life, Willa immediately drew back to Dawson. Her old life now found its way into the new.

I want to stop thinking about him, but I can't. Although we broke up, I think there is a chance we could get back together or at least hang out, but I'm worried about what my parents will say. Maybe I just won't tell them if it happens, but it probably won't.

As she forced the pen onto the textured paper, she purposefully marked her final period to indicate this thought process about Dawson had reached its end. Willa's cell phone buzzed beside her. It shook the carpet and her nerves. As she placed the pen down and closed the journal on top of it, Willa turned the phone to its face and saw the familiar name she had already missed.

"Rory, what's up?" Willa answered as she grinned. She rubbed the coarse carpet with her free hand and checked to see if Rory's voice came through the speakerphone. She could not stay still. She had wondered about Rory's well-being ever since her flight out of California. She had been too afraid to ask, though. Although Willa wanted Rory to tell her every detail about her date-gone-wrong as she had done with Rory, she knew it would never happen. At least not anytime soon.

"Hey, Willa," Rory responded softly. She seemed out of breath. "I just wanted to talk to you," she said painfully. Maybe she was just exhausted from surviving.

"What's wrong?" Willa knew by the sound of her voice she was not great.

"I'm actually doing pretty badly," she finally admitted. Her voice cracked, as it did every time before she cried. "I'm not sure why, but I started getting really bad headaches, and my chest hurts a lot. I think I'm just really stressed out, but I don't know what to do." She cried fully now and only took breaks in her sentences to sniffle. "I want to talk to someone."

"Tell your parents. You should go see a therapist or something, but if you decide you can't do that, you can always talk to me. I'm here for you, and I need you to know that, Ror. I'll always have your back." Willa said, relieved that Rory finally came to see her situation was far more serious than she had thought. "Just talk to *someone*."

"Okay, thanks. You know I want to tell you everything, Willa, but I just can't. I don't know how to explain," Rory held back the clenching in her throat and swallowed. "I have to go. I have to help my dad with something, but I'll talk to you soon, okay? Bye, Willa."

As Rory hung up, Willa placed her phone on the carpet. She knew Rory was headed toward healing. Telling someone was always a release. As she returned to her journal, her demeanor lightened, and her phone buzzed again. This time, it became one static buzz instead of a continuous chorus. When she looked down, thinking for a moment Rory's name would make a reappearance, she saw it was someone who had managed to replace all the worry that just left her body. She felt it now fill to the brim. Her chest felt tighter by the second, and her stomach fluttered.

Hey, Willa. This is Dawson. I know we haven't really talked in a while, but my sister heard you're home. Since we're both home, we should catch up sometime.

As she read this, Willa's curiosity ceased. Her question answered. Dawson was home for the summer.

CHAPTER THIRTY-ONE

———

The next morning, the first thing Willa did was check her phone. She reread Dawson's out of the blue message, and her stomach fluttered once again.

Hey, Willa. This is Dawson. I know we haven't really talked in a while, but my sister heard you're home. Since we're both home, we should catch up sometime.

He was right that they hadn't talked. For months, when Willa thought of him, she felt tempted to reach out, but she stopped herself. She did not want to trail back into a relationship she knew would consume her, no matter what she did. She told herself she would respond the day the message came in, but she could not bring herself to do so. Now, Willa typed and created a response that seemed untamable from the moment she typed the first letter to hitting send. Once it was gone, there was nothing she could do to stop it.

Sure, I'd love to.

With this small sentence, Willa revealed so much. Of course, part of her did want to see Dawson again, but she did not want to trudge through the awkwardness to normalcy. As her phone vibrated, a shock of nerves crawled under her skin.

Great! How about tonight at XXX Burgers at eight o'clock?

By the location, Willa knew this would be more than a casual encounter with an old friend. It was a date in a place they used to go often, and now, she realized what she had gotten herself into.

———

Willa listened to songs by the Dixie Chicks and reminisced on childhood memories as she got ready. She tried to calm herself. The one thing she was even more worried about was how she would navigate notifying her parents of her plans for the night. She was especially worried about her father, who would not care if Dawson went to college and had a great life or died in a ditch tomorrow because of how things ended. He did not appreciate how Dawson went against the original plan he and Willa had established, and he certainly did not appreciate the emotional rollercoaster Willa experienced.

When she realized her parents would find out one way or another, Willa decided to tell her mom, who would not take the news as harshly as she knew her dad would. Willa strolled into the living room and past her father, who claimed to be "resting his eyes," but had fallen into an intense slumber. She did not know how long he had been in this state, and she did not want to bother him. She sat next to her mother on the couch. As her mother watched the Home Network and beamed over people's home transformations, Willa decided to break the news slowly. She braced herself for her reply.

"Mom?" Willa asked gently. She tried to get her attention without rudely interrupting her TV time. Her mother held her hand up a few inches from Willa's mouth, and she frantically reached for the remote, so she could pause the program right before the climactic home reveal. Then, she turned to

Willa. She looked at her up and down and noticed Willa's rusty application of makeup. She also noticed Willa's outfit selection was nicer than usual.

"What is it?" she asked and tried to hide her smile.

"I'm going to hang out with Dawson tonight. Is that okay?"

The very second Willa spit out the word *Dawson*, her father woke up faster than she had ever seen.

"Who's hanging out with Dawson? Not you," he said immediately. He was clearly no longer in the mood to rest his eyes. He was ready to advocate for all the reasons Willa shouldn't spend any more time with the boyfriend he thought was long gone.

Her mother barged into the conversation before he could continue. "You know, Raymond," she said with a grin. "I think she should spend time with him if she wants to."

Both Willa and Raymond were surprised by her statement, and Raymond's posture quickly relaxed as he melted into the couch once again. He made it known he was still displeased by his stern facial expression, but he folded within himself.

"That's fine, I guess," he said, slightly irritated both from the subject of this conversation and from being woken up from his nap. "But he has to come over here and talk to *me* first."

————

Willa called Dawson twenty minutes before their meeting time and told him he had to talk with her parents before they could hang out. This was one of the most uncomfortable conversations Willa had ever had. Just thinking of the demand made her cringe.

"Hey, so, you need to come over to my house first and talk to my parents. That's fine, right?" she said.

"Sure, that's fine. I'll be there in like fifteen minutes," he replied and then hung up the phone, which left her heart beating rapidly. Her father was fully awake and ready to give Dawson a piece of his mind.

"It's not going to be good," Willa's mother said to her. Both of their bodies clenched. Her mother giggled with suspense and dread at the combination of the concerned look in her daughter's eyes and the steely expression on her husband's face.

For the remaining ten minutes of tension before Dawson would show his face on her father's property, Willa hid in her bedroom. She felt consumed with nerves. Her heart beat rapidly, her head pounded, and her limbs felt numb from concern and impatience.

She heard a car pull up in the driveway while the rain fell with force and drenched everything in sight.

Willa's mother called, "Willa, your little boyfriend is here." She laughed, and Raymond grew more irritated by his wife's response.

As she tiptoed through the hallway, Willa peeked her head around the corner and saw Dawson enter her house. His hair dripped with delicate raindrops, and his Converse squished with moisture.

"Hi, Mrs. Woodson," he said, shaking due to a combination of his clothing's stickiness and anxiety.

Before her mother could respond to Dawson's greeting, Willa's father barged through the hallway and to the front door. Willa still hid in the corner unseen, and she dug her nails into the wall and braced for what he would do.

"Raymond, don't be too dramatic." Her mother rolled her eyes and got out of the way, so he could move closer to Dawson.

"Hi, Mr. Woodson. How are you?" Dawson asked meekly. He moved his arms into his chest, unsure if he would be hit or hugged by the man who towered over him.

"I don't know if you guys are dating again or what," Willa's father began. "But this is the only time you will step foot in this house. I just wanted to speak with you and set things straight, but if you want to see my daughter, you can do it away from me. I can't control who she spends her time with because she's an adult now, but if I could, I wouldn't want her to see you again."

As she stepped out of her hiding place, Willa smiled from the awkwardness, as she always did. Dawson saw Willa and stared with fear and hurt in his eyes. This was even worse than when he had broken up with her.

"I get it, Mr. Woodson," he said and looked to Raymond's face and back to Willa's. "This won't be like the last time. I swear."

"Okay, bye!" Willa said sharply and grabbed Dawson's hand to lead him through the door to the outside world. While her father and mother stood there shocked, Willa and Dawson jumped into Dawson's car, then drove out of her neighborhood before they said a word.

CHAPTER THIRTY-TWO

—

As they drove away, Willa saw that Dawson gazed at her and smiled. They drove to a destination that resurrected fond memories for them both, and Willa was not quite sure how she felt.

They sat across from one another in a small booth suited for two. It was caked in grease and memories. To Willa's surprise, there was no moment of awkwardness or discomfort. They had settled back into their old routine. The two talked and laughed and almost felt as if they were never apart. It was like they had continued their relationship throughout college and had gotten together as they planned.

"You know, I've missed you a lot." Dawson smiled at her as she took a healthy bite of her veggie burger.

"I've missed you too. I am glad we are doing this," she responded after a big swallow.

As she watched him, she chuckled under his breath and flashed his smile Willa had once known like the back of her own hand. She ached for him no matter how much she tried to resist. She did not know if he longed for her in the same way or if he simply wanted to get together and catch up after a year apart. She believed she had finally made strides toward moving on, but at this moment, she fell back into her old ways.

———

After they ate, Dawson and Willa sat in a park filled with moments of their time together. *Why is he taking me to these places?* They both sat in the open trunk of his car and looked at the view of the sunset after the rain cleared. At last, they began the topic she'd dreaded for the entirety of the day— their relationship.

Dawson turned to face Willa instead of the outside world. "So," he said shakily. "Do you want to talk about what this is?"

The vagueness and confusion in his proposal made her more unsure of what they were than before.

"Well, I don't really know." She tried to sound unfazed. "I'm not going to lie that when you asked me to hang out, I thought you meant more like a date, but if this is just a friend thing, then that's fine too." Willa's heart thumped inside her chest, but on the outside, she remained collected.

"To be honest... I still have feelings for you."

Those were words she had not dared to expect but had secretly hoped for the night before. She had imagined them vividly in her dreams, so she teased a quiet smile.

"I still have feelings for you too."

Before they could exchange soft glances, Dawson made a declaration.

"I don't want to be in a relationship, though." He turned slightly away from Willa and looked at his tattered shoes. "If we were to do this, I would be down to probably hook up and hang out. Nothing too serious, you know?"

He looked at her plainly as he waited for Willa's response. Strangely, she was not surprised by this. Although they had dedicated their romantic feelings to one another for two whole years and now reconnected, it did not surprise her that Dawson had decided to play it safe. In a way, she was glad, she supposed. With this arrangement, Willa would not get her heartbroken again.

"Okay, I would be fine with that." The straight line of her lips cracked into a grin, even though she felt no real happiness.

———

That night, Willa was nervous because she had not been with anyone since Raimy. And even then, she had not been with him in this way.

The two moved to the inside of Dawson's car since they had nowhere else to go. As Willa watched Dawson under the light of the summer moon and streetlamps, she knew she was in a vulnerable situation. She believed this would be fine, but now she saw him like this, and her feelings returned. She was uncertain.

To kiss him again for the first time felt familiar, as though they had never stopped. As he smiled and held her, Willa felt happy. *I love him.*

She realized she knew from the moment she saw his name appear on her phone screen. She still felt this way. But even though they had shared experiences such as this, as love circled through the muggy car air, he no longer loved her the same way. It was something she could not explain but felt. That was a fact she had to deal with, and she needed to make sure he did not break her as he had done before. Willa had to turn this tragedy of love, loss, and love again into something casual. It was a relationship that benefited them both, to an extent, but broke one of their hearts without the other's knowledge. Willa was in for an unforgettable summer, no matter how desperately she wanted to forget.

CHAPTER THIRTY-THREE

——

As they laid down on the grass one afternoon, Dawson and Willa laughed and talked as they always did. However, despite how they spent two days a week together, both knew the summer would end. The beginning of August was a reminder Dawson left for school in two short weeks.

To spend the summer with Dawson was a mixture of both pleasure and pain. On the one hand, Willa loved being with him. They did everything they used to. They went to bookstores and found memoirs, which Willa loved dearly, and they searched for the best vegetarian restaurants in the area. Also, they spend time outside in parks or on hikes, just to feel the clean air against their skin. Dawson's pale cheeks would always turn the pink of cherry blossoms, and Willa's usual rose lips would shiver to plum.

"I don't want to leave," he said plainly. He sat up while Willa lay on her back. Her neck and head rested upon his upper thigh, and her skin scratched against the seam of his jeans.

"Why?" Willa twisted grass in between her pointer finger and thumb.

"I like spending time with you, but…" Willa could tell by the sudden silence he wanted to craft the perfect sentence to speak aloud. "I don't think I can do this anymore. Leaving will be too hard if we see each other on the last day before I go. I don't want to leave, obviously, but since I am, I think we should probably have time apart."

She processed his statement. Then she sat up and looked him dead in the eyes the same way she had done one year ago. He made the face he did when he knew Willa was upset. He understood there was nothing he could do to fix it. This made the most sense.

"I'm really sorry, Willa," he said with a shrug. Willa was unable to determine if his apology was sincere or not. "This is kind of out of the blue, but I don't want to get hurt again, so I think this should be the last time we hang out before I go back to school."

I don't want to get hurt again. Neither did Willa, but she still wanted to spend time with Dawson while they had the chance.

"Alright." She shielded her emotions. "If that's what you want to do."

———

After she said goodbye to Dawson for the last time for what would be months or longer, they stood in front of her door, where he'd dismissed her love for the first time. He did not seem angry with himself for doing this to Willa again. He looked rather numb. To her, it seemed he did not care in the same way he once had, and she was the one who got hurt.

"I'll see you when we get home for Thanksgiving or Christmas?" he asked, and she nodded. She did not know if she wanted to see him again, to spend an amazing month together and be bluntly abandoned once more.

She gave Dawson a half-hearted hug and watched as he turned away. He walked farther and farther from her. When she told her parents, they were happy he was gone. They were glad he was out of her life, even if only for a short while.

"You know, Willa. I think you can do better," her mother said to her bluntly that night. They sat beside one another as they ate stovetop popcorn and watched their favorite film, *Pretty Woman*.

From the memories Willa held so close to her heart, Dawson seemed great. He felt like someone she would never want to lose. But after she replayed the constant dismissal of her feelings and how his love dissipated through every interaction, she asked herself if she could do better. Willa's mother knew it was likely, and now, she did too.

Sitting there, with her eyes glued on the television screen, she thought about her mother's words and decided not to see Dawson again. This was a decision she would stand by despite the temptation. Although it was easier said than done, and a lingering part of her still wanted to share her life and heart with him, she knew she deserved better, and now, she had to be patient until she believed wholeheartedly.

PART FOUR:

LOSING

CHAPTER THIRTY-FOUR:

EMI

Thirty-two years after Emi's story:

Once their children grew into adults with lives of their own, Sonny and Emi traveled more. In the early years of their independence, after Jo and Milo moved away to attend college and beyond, Sonny and Emi drove to faraway states and explored the natural miracles America provided more frequently. For Sonny, it was the first time he had traveled in this way. He had never left the restraints of his small town until college and considered these places so foreign. Sonny exhibited a childlike excitement when they would drive for hours. This had always been a dream of his, and it was finally coming true.

As the two got older, they traveled less. Emi was in her late fifties, and Sonny crept into his sixties. Sonny spoke to her about the future one night in the kitchen as he helped Emi prepare dinner. The two of them danced along to his favorite soul album, which scratched against the ancient record player. Sonny claimed it was in "perfect condition" and these new "music listening devices" on the market would never compare to his own old-fashioned system. As their dancing began to slow and the music shifted from one track to the next, he began to speak, slowly and softly close to her right ear.

"I know we haven't been traveling as much lately, but we're both getting older, Emi. Let's go on one of our fishing trips that we haven't done in months. What about Idaho, just a state away? It'll be fun and good for us to get out of this house."

Emi knew he was right, even though his record of having such brilliant ideas was far less consistent than her own.

"I agree," she said with a sigh. "But we aren't *that* old. You make it sound like we're on our deathbed."

The two laughed, and as she turned toward her cutting board that rested upon the countertop and prepared to chop three hardy onions, Sonny smiled and pulled her frail body toward his steady one. His grin filled the entirety of his face, and his eyes sparkled.

"This will be fun, just the two of us," he said and released her from his chest. He returned to wash lettuce and later left Emi to finish the meal.

———

As Emi sat in their folding chairs, she sipped Sonny's signature sweet tea recipe with extra lemon. Sonny threw his fishing line in and out of the open water. His dark eyes glistened from the reflection of the lake and shined up onto his face. It created a glow on his skin with tones of browns, oranges, and blues. His complexion was an August sunset.

Even though Emi enjoyed these trips, she despised the concept of fishing. She'd never understood the point of bothering these poor fish who lived in the water. None of them paid any mind to the humans above the surface, and she felt badly when they were caught, but Sonny absolutely adored it, and because of this fact, she said nothing. Nothing made him happier than to exist in the quiet and watch as Emi read a book or wrote in her journal. He would carry his fishing rod high and sit beside her.

He always hoped he would become lucky and capture a fish big enough to fill both of their bellies for dinner. Bragging to his old friends in the neighborhood about his accomplishments would be such fun. Emi made an effort to love what Sonny loved, and Sonny made an effort to love what Emi loved. That was the reason these trips always brought excitement to both of their lives. They both loved to watch one another do what they loved, and that was why they loved each other.

As they sat by the water for a few days, they read books and caught fish in the morning and afternoon. They fried them up in the RV by night. As Sonny waited patiently for the fish to bite, Emi noticed his gaze shifted, and he seemed unfocused. He often looked away while Emi read her book. Meanwhile, the words on the page quickly became meaningless, and her mind continued to race. Her thoughts spun as she tried to think of an explanation.

After a week of needed relaxation, they cleared their heads. Emi sat beside Sonny in the front seats of their RV. Sonny preferred to drive along the winding roads and amongst the tall trees and vast mountains, and Emi preferred to read. When Emi was halfway through her story and about ready to flip the page, Sonny looked at her with his peripheral vision.

"Emi?" he asked softly.

Emi replied with a simple grunt, to imply she would close her book in a moment, but then he began to speak.

"I know you feel fine, and that's great, but I think you should go to the doctor sometime next week. Just to get a checkup," he said casually. He turned his focus back to the road as soon as he posed the question.

"Why do you think I should do that?" Emi asked slowly. She pressed her fingers harder between the pages now, blindsided by this comment. Sonny was nervous and held a feeling in his chest that Emi had not taken this suggestion lightly. He placed his right hand upon the point of her left knee and reached as far as he could to provide her with comfort.

"That book you are reading," he began, and he turned his head slightly and looked at how far along she was in the novel. "You usually read a book that size in two or three days on these trips, but I've seen you going back a few pages and forgetting your place entirely. I'm just worried you might be getting more confused. That never happens to you... never."

It was true it had taken her longer to get through this three-hundred-page book. Without realizing it, Emi had gone back a few pages here and there, but it did not feel abnormal to her. *It's probably just my age that's affecting my memory.* This felt like a decent explanation.

"I appreciate your concern, honey, but I'm fine." She placed her hand on top of his. "I'm not going to the doctor. I don't need to."

Sonny knew what Emi was doing. He did not want to embarrass her or make her feel worse. Ever since they'd decided Emi would not work, upon the reveal of her second pregnancy, Emi never searched for work again. Sometimes Sonny felt she had never fully forgiven him for holding her to the shackles of their own home. Her only career was defined by cooking recipes out of a book and the number of times she cleaned the white-tiled floor of the bathroom per week.

"Okay, that's fine," he said, and he lowered his voice in regret. He lifted his hand to remove it from under Emi's and returned it back to the vast steering wheel. Sonny returned his gaze to the long road that carried them from one state of the vast Pacific Northwest to another.

Emi returned to her book and stared at the words, which appeared to become less meaningful in her mind. After she looked at a page full of sentences and searched for a story within them, she flipped back to the beginning of the chapter and read once again.

Sonny saw the wheels of her mind turn, and a frost of disorientation glossed over her. Even so, he did not say another word.

CHAPTER THIRTY-FIVE:

WILLA

———

When Willa returned to school for her second year, she was ready for it, and she was eager to reinvent herself. She felt the jolt of the landing plane and heard the tires skid against the pavement. And she found the familiar faces of people who went to the same school, but she did not know well enough to approach. Excitement rushed over Willa as she fetched her bags and made her way back to campus. Willa could not wait to see Rory. She had thought of her often and longed for her dearly, and now, the time for them to reconnect was here.

Willa walked the halls of an old dorm building. It was caked with dust and already wafted a scent of weed and incense. She struggled to open the door as she carried a hefty suitcase in one hand. Once the door opened, she saw Rory, seated on their old thrift store couch. She laughed as she watched funny videos on the television. When she saw Willa, she jumped up to attack Willa with an embrace.

"I missed you so much, you bitch," Rory joked and nearly knocked Willa over with the force of her grasp.

Willa dropped her belongings in their shared room, just outside of the common area, then walked back to the couch to sit next to Rory and discuss everything that had happened during their time apart.

"Do you remember that whole thing that happened to me last year? You know, the dating thing?" Rory asked. She set her phone down on the side table and wrapped her arms around herself lightly. She appeared more comfortable now, but her body was a bit tense.

Willa was unsure if they would ever talk about this again, especially since she had refused to talk about it in depth before.

"Yeah," Willa responded in a reserved voice. "What about it? Are you okay?"

"I'm fine. I ended up telling my parents and getting help, actually, which was nice."

Willa had not scorned her, but she was happy Rory had told someone.

"I'm proud of you, Rory. That's great." Willa reached in for another embrace, and this time, Rory rested her head upon Willa's shoulder and squeezed her a bit tighter.

———

As they talked more about Willa's life in the last three months, she skirted the topic of her love life. She did not want Dawson to make his way into the conversation, but naturally, she knew he would.

"What about that guy from back home? Dawson, right?" Rory asked with a smile. She probably thought everything had gone well.

"Actually, that's kind of over for good. We ended up hanging out for most of the summer, but he just didn't feel the same way anymore, I don't think. He said he missed me and everything, but I don't know. It just felt different, I guess."

"Well, I'm sorry it didn't work out," she responded, and Willa leaked a soft smile to indicate she was pleased with her apology and felt the same. "Based on what you said, he seemed like a great guy. That's really too bad."

Willa was disappointed this relationship had not lived up to its once great expectations, but after their time apart, she did not know what she expected.

"It's alright. I deserve better." Willa said.

Rory nodded in complete agreement. "You sure do."

CHAPTER THIRTY-SIX:

EMI

—

After Emi and Sonny's fishing endeavor, Emi's mind escaped her more frequently than before. When she returned to her everyday activities to cook, clean, and worry about her children from a distance, the memory lapses persisted. It began with reading, as she forgot her place and skipped back to prior pages. Then, she began to forget to prepare meals and where she had placed things. Once, she forgot Sonny's name.

Even though Emi became worse as the weeks progressed, Sonny acted as if everything was normal. He still did not want to offend her or hurt her feelings, but his worry escalated when Emi started to forget *him*. It was scary when she looked at this man she had known better than herself, with no recollection and no memory of over thirty years spent together. He was devastated.

When Emi and Sonny went to bed one night, Sonny checked all the locked doors and turned off every light, except for the one in their bedroom. Emi had already fallen asleep. Her body was so still that Sonny often placed his face directly above hers and waited to hear her breath.

"Goodnight, my love," he whispered before he closed his eyes. This phrase was unwavering, whether Emi was awake or asleep. He smiled and felt his wife's warm body beside him, excited for the day they would spend together tomorrow.

As Sonny awoke the following morning, he moved his arm up and down Emi's frame. When she woke up, she jumped up from his touch. She screamed with fear in her eyes. Emi pushed Sonny off of her immediately, and tears flowed out of her undeniable fear.

"Help!" she yelled, ran away, and bumped into her grand bookshelf, the corner of counters, and even the legs of chairs and tables, which scraped the hardwood.

"Emi, calm down!" Sonny ran after her, but his large presence only made her more fearful.

"Stop, please! Don't hurt me," she pleaded. Once she said that, he stopped in his tracks. Every one of his limbs grew weak, and he cried. Finally, pulling himself together and pressing Emi's arms to her side in a hold, he knew this could not continue.

"Emi," he said slowly, to try and calm her jittery emotions and make her look at him, if only for a moment. "I am your husband, Sonny. You just woke up confused, but let's go back to bed, okay? You need to rest, and I'm not going to hurt you. You're just having trouble remembering."

The more Sonny tried to comfort her with his words and constant explanation, the calmer Emi became. Her body relaxed, and with her eyes fogged from exhaustion, she returned to bed. Sonny tucked her under the covers comfortably and then moved to leave her in the bedroom alone, wiping his own eyes as he left. When Emi looked at him and the memories trickled back in time, she could not help but feel bad for what she had done and how painful it must be for him. When she peered through the windows of his eyes, she saw nothing.

"Sonny?" she said underneath the covers as he left. His head swiveled to her quickly, and a sparkle of hope ignited within his face.

"I'm sorry. I think I was just confused." She lifted her head to see him more clearly. Once she finished speaking, she set herself back down along her pillow.

"I know," he sighed. "We can talk about this when you wake up."

———

While Emi lay in bed with him the following night, she read slowly. Sonny turned to her and closed his newspaper. He placed the paper on his side table and freed both of his arms to wrap them around her. His eyes were like the ocean's abyss and filled with tears. Water brimmed to the top of his eye sockets and overflowed, and the wetness of his cheeks faded his skin and enhanced their ash undertone.

"I don't want you to leave me," he whispered with tenderness.

Emi could do nothing to ease his pain and to ease her own. Her memory, her inability to recognize the abnormality within her own behavior, pried her away from the most important person in her world.

"I'm not going to leave you," Emi said and felt a prickling within her throat, as it always touched her in the most fragile place when she saw Sonny weep. "With your name and my eyes, we could brighten up this whole world."

This only made the two of them cry harder. They knew, together, they filled each other's lives with light. He brightened up her world, her universe, and the light to his world now dimmed.

"Can you please just go to the doctor?" he asked softly. He could no longer spare her feelings and ached with selfishness.

"Yes," Emi said, and she moved her hands from his hips to his soft cheeks. Her slim fingers wiped away his great pool of tears. "For you."

CHAPTER THIRTY-SEVEN:

WILLA

A month into school, everything was going far better than Willa imagined. She and Rory remained inseparable, and they paid no mind to Raimy. However, Willa decided to withdraw from the environmental club because of the awkwardness and recurring memories. Since this was Willa's second year in college, she felt relieved because she knew how to stay on track with academics and still have fun in the process.

When Dawson reached out to Willa again a month into the new school year, she finally came to terms with their bitter end and discovered the truth of just how much better she was without him. This reappearance occurred late into the night while she did her homework. She was already too concerned about the math class she struggled in and did not have time to think about possible love interests, old or new.

Hey, Willa. It's Dawson. I just wanted to see how you are doing and if you are going to be in town, I'm excited to hang out with you during Thanksgiving break :)

Willa looked at the face of her phone the minute it buzzed, then groaned as she scribbled the answer to one of her math problems in her tattered notebook. She did not want to talk to Dawson anymore, did not want to hang out with him again, and this message was the final test to see if she would remain true to her word. She had finally reached a point where she no longer had butterflies. She no longer felt the buzzing in her limbs from excitement. She only felt pure disinterest. Although she thought of a day where they could be friends, she was certain now was the wrong time.

Hey. I think I'm going to be pretty busy over Thanksgiving with family stuff. Maybe another time.

Maybe another time. A phrase used to reject those who need to be let down gently. Willa had finally released her answer into the world that reflected her true feelings. She no longer looked forward to seeing Dawson as she did the past summer. Now, she had closed the lingering hope of a relationship between them. Dawson had been brought up to speed with how things would go from now on. Maybe another time means never.

Alright, just let me know.

Willa looked at his text and did not reply. She did not feel the need to give him potential hope that no longer lived between them. It was over, and after she read his quick response, she closed her phone and did not think about him again. She continued her math homework as if the conversation had never happened, and she felt lighter. A weight lifted off of her shoulders, which she had felt bearing down on her for years.

As she lay on her bed and worked on her homework, her phone blared. Its ring nearly burned the hairs inside of her ears with its piercing screech. Only one person she knew would call in these unpredictable hours, so she answered quickly,

"Mom? What's up?" Willa asked, and her voice gurgled from her heavy breath.

For a while, she said nothing. She heard pants through the phone speaker as her mother's stress became hers. "You have to come home, just for a week." She did not want to cry in front of the one person she needed to protect. "Your grandfather," she said. "It's sudden, but he became really sick this past week, Willa. You have to visit him in the hospital. We aren't sure yet, but if you don't come soon, it might be too late."

Willa sat beside her grandfather and heard the inhales and exhales of a ventilator, which hung above him like a chandelier. She held his hand, and his fingers were dry and cracked.

"Hi, Grandpa," Willa said softly, a bit self-conscious that people in the hallway could hear. "It's Willa."

He did not move or flinch or extend a single finger. She looked at the face that had always been filled with soul and power. It already looked lifeless. His color remained rich, but his lips were pale and peeled. His eyes were closed beneath dark and hollow lids. He meant the world to Willa and even more to her mother and grandmother. He was the sun to all their skies and the light that dazzled any dark day, and now he was dimming in front of them.

Willa saw her grandmother stroll in as her mother held her thin arm to keep her stable. Her face looked the same as it had for months now. It was empty at times. And every time Willa saw her, she never knew what state to expect.

"Hello," her grandmother said and then placed her hand on Sonny's leg and stared. She did not cry. There was not even a crack in her voice or sign of weakness. It was as if she sat before this man who she did not know, who was unrecognizable to her, but showed affection as she felt she had to.

As the doctor walked in, she gave Willa's grandmother and mother both a look of pity. "Can we get everyone in here, please? I think we know what the issue is."

Willa's mother, father, uncle, and aunt all rushed in, then stood around the room as the one in the white coat bared his future.

"Unfortunately, he has leukemia. I'm so sorry, but it is too late in the development, so there is nothing we can do to really treat him."

Everyone looked around in distress and sorrow as tears filled their eyes. They ran down Willa's cheeks and onto her fingers, which pressed against his. This was the man she went on trips with every summer to fish and hike and even go to waterparks. The one who filled her belly with the richest foods and introduced her to so many wonders in life. He was the only man she'd ever loved unconditionally other than her own father. There was nothing they could do, and certainly, there was nothing Willa could do. Through all the chaos, as everyone tried to cope, Willa looked at her grandmother.

Nothing.

Her face was unreadable, and she had not shifted since before she heard the news. She did not cry. She gazed around the room, and her mouth gaped, unconcerned. She did not seem to understand why everyone was so upset.

CHAPTER THIRTY-EIGHT:

JO

The fear buried in Sonny's eyes the night Willa came home was an image Jo would never forget. It fueled her concern for what had happened between him and her mother. Although she had not noticed anything different, besides her father's demeanor and denial of any changes or news he should inform her of, Jo's worry grew stronger for her mother. She recognized Sonny only presented this type of worry concerning Emi's problems, not his own, and Jo was fearful to ask her mother if anything had happened. She did not want to be the one to unveil her father's concerns when Jo was unsure if her mother even knew the nature of them.

When Jo was home, she felt spoiled by how easy it had been with so many extra hands. Now, she and Raymond were alone with Willa to fend for themselves. With just Raymond and Jo, they could no longer rest in moments where they began to break, with the knowledge their baby was taken care of by those they trusted most.

Throughout their stay back in Jo's childhood home, Jo's mother was the most eager to help. There was nothing she loved more than children. She always glowed when she walked past any child and discussed with Jo what she thought their dreams and aspirations would be.

"When you were younger," Emi said to Jo in almost every conversation related to children, "I knew you wanted to work in fashion, to make some kind of clothing, or write about clothing. You always had the *eye*."

Even though Jo highly doubted her mother seriously knew this for the duration of her childhood, she'd learned early on her mother loved to talk about Jo's childhood love for clothing. When Jo and her mother discussed what *she* dreamed of being when she was young, her mother always grew quiet. The very mention of anything about her childhood spawned unease. She never told Jo of any of her dreams, except those related to Sonny and her children.

"The only dream I have," she would always begin, "is that you, Milo, and your father are happy and healthy. And the four of us continue to show each other love."

———

Jo knew she would never be able to pry information from her father's mouth, so he went to her brother. Sonny was always stubborn and kept things that did not concern her to himself.

Jo drove to see Milo, just an hour away from the home of their childhood. Once she arrived, she was greeted by him. He was concerned about why she had wanted to talk to him so suddenly, unsure of what the conversation would entail. Jo sat across from him on his kitchen counter, and she stared at Penny as she prepared ingredients for seafood gumbo, Milo's favorite meal. Milo waited for her to bring up the topic she felt they needed to discuss.

"You know when we all stayed at Ma and Dad's when I first brought Willa home from the hospital?" Jo began. Milo leaned in slightly. "Well, did you notice Dad acting differently? He seemed to be worried about Ma."

Milo's face did not change. He broke into a slight chuckle a few seconds later. "I sort of noticed, but I don't think it's anything... She's just getting older. Both of them are."

He was right, she supposed. They were both getting older, and time never seemed to do great favors.

"Yeah, I guess. Never mind, it's probably nothing. I'm just a little worried, that's all."

"It's sweet that you're concerned, Joey," Milo responded as he stepped a bit closer to his sister. He put one of his hands on her shoulder. "Want to stay for dinner? I'm sure that we'll have enough."

"No, I think I am okay, actually," Jo said casually. She felt an overwhelming desire to be alone. "I think I'll probably stop and get a burger on my way home. That sounds pretty good to me right now, actually."

"Okay, well, you and Raymond are welcome over here for dinner, or just if you want to talk anytime. You know that," he finished. Both he and Penny walked Jo out their front door. They watched as she climbed into her car and left them, then drove away into the evening smog. They smelled the crisp scent from the clouds and knew it was about to rain.

Jo pulled into an old parking lot. Rain trickled upon her windshield, and she already smelled the oil and cheese from inside the diner she and Milo used to frequent growing up. They were always confident their fries and chocolate milkshakes would be delicious.

As she got out of her car and stepped into the building, the wet rubber of her soles squeaked against the old tile from the early 1970s. She walked up to the high bar counter and sat in a worn revolving chair, then rubbed her fingers against the wrinkles and rips. She grinned as the juvenile memories rushed back to her.

"Hi, sweetie. What can I get ya?" a burly woman asked. She wore a ruffled apron and a tired smile. Her skin reeked of grease, but the smell only caused Jo's stomach to ache more ferociously with hunger.

"Hi," Jo responded with a polite grin. She looked up from the menu. "May I please get your chili cheeseburger with fries and a chocolate shake?"

"Sure thing, doll. We'll have that out for you in just a bit." The woman took the menu from Jo and pranced away. The force of her hips swinging caused the ruffles on her outfit to move along with them.

Jo looked around. The fluorescent lights stung her eyes. She gazed upon the happy faces and conversations among families and friends. Jo could not help but worry about her mother, no matter how hard she tried to distract herself. She had been stuck in her own spiraling thoughts of what-ifs. The only feeling that cascaded over her body was the prick of worry. As Jo continued to spiral, she noticed the aching of hunger deep in her stomach had gone away and been entirely placed with her worried tingling. She was broken out of her haze by a voice she could not place a face to but recognized.

"Jo? Jo Sanders?"

Jo twisted her chair around.

"Hi?" She knew she had seen this face before but was unsure of where and when.

"You don't remember me, do you?" The man chuckled slightly to cover his embarrassment.

"I'm really sorry, but I don't quite remember. How do I know you?" Jo asked, then reached out her hand for him to shake. He did and grinned. Jo felt a spark of nostalgia in his piercing eyes.

"Phil Foster, but in college, everybody called me Philly." He looked intently at Jo's face to see if that had ignited any recognition. Her expression remained unchanged. "Johnny set us up back in the day. We went on one date at a bar, I think," he said, and he reflected upon the date as if it had gone amazingly, but as Jo looked at him, it all swarmed back in a sudden instant.

"Oh, I remember you," Jo said sourly, then pulled away from Philly slightly. His eyebrows recoiled in response. "You're the one who ran away like a little bitch when my ex-boyfriend punched me in the face."

As she barked her reply and held nothing back, Philly no longer looked pleased to see Jo. He looked terrified.

"Yeah... but that was a long time ago, Jo," he stuttered. "We're fine *now*, right?" He leaned in closer as if he expected an immediate hug.

Jo leaned away. "I can forgive, Philly, and I forgave you a long time ago. But I will never forget. Trust me, I've tried. I would appreciate it if you would leave now. I hope you have a great night." She was no longer taken over by her frustration toward Philly's action long ago. Instead, she was crippled by the memories it had provoked. She did not want to think about that time in her life, what Apollo had done to her, and the damage she had done to herself because of it.

"Well, I hope you have a great night too, Jo. You deserve it."

"Yeah," Jo responded awkwardly and turned away from a man who meant nothing to her. He was a person who brought forth painful memories, and for that, she never wanted to see him again.

"Well, sweetie, just in time. I was worried you were gonna talk to that friend of yours for ages, and I didn't want your food to get too cold." The waitress walked up to Jo's place at the counter, then placed down her meal. She appeared livelier this time around.

"Thank you," Jo whispered politely as she saw her food. The steam filled her nostrils and made her mouth water. "But he's not a friend. Just a bad memory."

CHAPTER THIRTY-NINE:

EMI

Emi sat on an uncomfortable bench, and the wrinkling of thin examination table paper scratched at the bottoms of her bare thighs. Sonny was directly across from her and sat in a wooden chair as he stared. He attempted to guess the diagnosis before given to either one of them.

In this process, the doctor gave Emi many tests. Originally, they made little sense to her, but later, she explained them in a way that appeared less intimidating than she initially felt.

"Emi, if you want to come with me, we are just going to take a couple of tests. They are like fun games that test your memory, how fast you can think of answers, methods to solve problems, and things of that sort. Does that sound okay?" the doctor questioned as she sat directly across from Emi.

This time, it was clear Sonny was not allowed in the room. As they changed location and Sonny remained seated in the original space, the doctor led Emi to her office and sat a bit closer. "Okay, ready to get started?" the doctor asked, and Emi felt a strong sense of calm.

"Sure," Emi responded. Today, she felt more alive than she had in days, and this gave her hope.

"All right then," the doctor began, then placed her clipboard in front of her and peered up at her. Her eyes were bigger now, and the both of them sat up straight. "Let's get started. Can you tell me what the season is? Is it fall, winter, spring, or summer?"

———

Emi's head pounded from all the questions, but it was finally complete. Emi now did everything Sonny had begged her so desperately to do, but she did not feel any relief when it was over. No matter what the results were, once Emi walked out of the evaluation, Sonny remained concerned. He still shook in his boots. He felt scared of what information lay on the other side. One single person contained a message that would alter both Emi and Sonny's lives eternally.

"How did it go?" he asked as Emi strolled back to him and wrapped her arms around his thick body. He held on loosely and slouched from fatigue.

"I think it went well," she responded, and then they sat in silent anticipation.

When the doctor walked in, she broke the elongated silence in the room. The doctor looked discouraged, even a bit saddened, but she tried to look calm.

"We looked over all of your results from the testing we did earlier, and it is not as good as we had hoped," she said slowly, looking at Emi intently. He seemed too afraid to do the same with Sonny. Her long hands grasped onto her clipboard, and her small-framed glasses slipped off her nose as she tilted her head downward.

No matter what the results were, Emi did not mind nearly as much as Sonny did. As she spoke, the doctor expected a more devastating expression from Emi's face. Tears had already begun to fall from her husband's eyes. "It appears you have early onset Alzheimer's disease. Now, are either of you familiar with this?"

Emi had only ever heard about it in vague terms. Sonny was slightly familiar with it himself, and that faint recognition only made him cry harder. He jolted his body up and down and puffed foreign sounds.

"Alzheimer's is a progressive disease that ultimately weakens your memory and other functions over time. As of now, it is irreversible."

Emi remained still. She no longer looked at Sonny but at the floor. It was an off-white color with specks of varying primary tones within it. It had dark streaks from shoes worn on other patients. Those streaks indicated others had sat in this very room and also heard their same depressing fate.

"How much time?" she asked. "Before, I don't remember anything?" Saying this only made Sonny release more sounds of pain, and he now tapped into an emotion more profound than agony. It freed itself through cracks and wheezes, and his tears fell faster. His hands shielded his eyes to keep others from witnessing the full state of his misery.

"I'm not sure. I don't think any of us can be. The process is different for everyone, but I would say just be present at this moment. Be in the *now,* and try not to worry about the rest, though I understand this is much easier said than done."

Emi was not worried about the rest. As a person who had lived an unconventional life that differed from her family's expectations, she'd never feared death or the direction her life was headed now. She felt it was all planned, even if this plan was not her own.

As the doctor walked out of the room, she placed a single hand upon Sonny's shoulder. He cried and shielded his face as he bent over.

"Are you okay?" Emi asked as the door clicked shut, but she knew the answer.

"I just don't want you to go. This is all too soon," he sobbed, unable to look at his wife because he knew it would only make him cry harder.

"I'll never be *gone.*" She smiled in an effort to brighten his mood. "As long as I love you, you'll love me, *right?*" Emi perked up.

"Of course, I will," he responded, then stood and walked over to her. He pushed her face into the dip of his chest. His palms and fingers were wet from his tears, and Emi felt the stickiness of droplets on the thin collar of his cotton shirt.

"Good." She tucked deeper into his chest now. "Then we'll be fine."

As she was slowly released from his embrace, Emi's mind no longer spun with the worries of Sonny but of Jo and Milo. What would they think of this, and how would they react? She did not know but had a feeling it would not blow over well.

Unafraid of death, Emi never thought of the consequences. She never delved into just how memory loss would separate her from herself and what made her the person she was today. To no longer remember her own daughter and son was an outcome even worse than death. Emi's new fear had shown its face.

Looking into her daughter's eyes, flecked with green and brown and her son's near black, the two had come from her. Emi thought of her family, the family that had abandoned her at her lowest of times and realized all at once that soon she would not recall any of it. She hoped and prayed to anyone who listened that she would die before it came to that point, because then, she felt as though her life would not be worth living at all. Even forgetting the most painful parts of her past would mean to forget, and although it could bring peace, she did not want all that would come with it. She did not want to forget anything, not her painful past, and especially not her children.

"What will we tell the kids?" Emi asked, but Sonny could not satisfy her with an adequate answer. He shrugged, wiped his last drop from his round cheek, and grabbed his wife's hands before he pulled them up to his soft lips and kissed them.

"Let's just not tell them until after Jo gives birth and everything calms down." Emi knew Sonny was right. They should wait. And that is exactly what they did.

CHAPTER FORTY

Willa and her mother drove among the pine trees, and aged snow still sparkled from branches in the cold and crisp air. Willa gazed out of the window while thoughts roamed her mind, and Jo stared straight forward. Jo's face held a look of nervousness and anxiety as she followed along the winding path. Between them was silence.

They walked through the open doors of a small house as the aroma of freshly grown tomatoes and warm chocolate chip cookies snaked around the outside corners and into their noses. Willa had not visited her grandmother for over two years, and she knew the life-filled eyes she recalled from her earliest memories would no longer contain that same sparkle. There was no longer a light in them. Combined with her smile, it lit up a room, even when steeped in the angriest of moods.

Willa had known, no matter how much she and her mother pretended it would be the same as it always was, things changed. She carried a feeling that both of them would continue to stare at someone they loved unconditionally but would never have that love reciprocated. They would gawk at eyes that looked back at them with no hint of recollection left in them, despite the empty home.

Sitting in a room that screamed of dusty pink and eggshell white, Jo and Willa sat close to one another. Their hands did not touch, but their rings mingled. Jo wore her emerald wedding ring, and Willa's hand was full of rings in rose and white golds, which provided support to varying-sized jade stones. Both of them loved green, and it seemed to flatter their fingers in the best way. They slouched and waited, and they created polite small talk with the wrinkled and confused patients who strolled around the halls with the support of their walkers and helpers. Ten minutes had gone by.

Jo moved her hands onto the table, twiddling her thumbs, and Willa looked over her right shoulder toward an old television. She admired the 1940s western film that played on low volume. It was ignored by all who slept or ate in front of it except for her, who held a focused admiration.

Emerald looked at both Willa and Jo, who turned their attentions toward her, with welcoming smiles plastered on their faces. Standing up now, out of the thin wooden seats that grew uncomfortable, Willa and Jo both made way to Emi. They helped her sit down in the stiff wooden seat. Hers was made more comfortable by a thin rose cushion.

"Hi, Ma." Jo lifted her voice an octave as if she spoke to a dog or a child.

Willa leaned forward to give Emi a delicate, unreciprocated hug. "Hi, Grandma. How are you?"

No response. There was only an answer from the young face behind her.

"She's doing really well. A bit sad lately, but she'll be alright."

Emi did not look as sad as the woman who hovered above described her, but instead, she looked confused. The expression seemed normal for Emi now. Emi stared at the two women in front of her. Jo had the green flecks in her eyes, and Willa had long soft curls. Everyone in that room knew they had to be related. They all radiated the same beauty. It was the type of beauty only found in the 1960s fashion magazines Jo used to awe over. She looked at these astoundingly elegant women with thick hair and eyes as big and round as a doll's.

What upset Jo the most was when Emi talked about Sonny.

"Where is Sonny? Is he doing alright?" she asked randomly when she had been silent for the entirety of the visit.

When Emi asked this, life would flash back into her face. The dull spaces would begin to brighten, and her high-yellow cheeks flushed to scarlet. This is what made Jo the most upset, even though she was the only one who felt this way. Although Emi looked excited for a moment, it would all vanish into the soiled Depends-thickened air when Jo broke the same news again.

"No, Ma. Dad died from leukemia a few *years ago*."

Sonny's death now felt like a distant memory, and this sentence brought a weight upon all three of their hearts. It was a continuous reminder of what they had lost, and this made it harder to forget.

———

After Sonny's diagnosis, he had only twelve days left of his life. Emi's memory had taken a downward plunge no one expected. When she stood there at the funeral, still able to carry a conversation and show the remnants of her personality,

Jo watched her look into the vast hole dug in the cold February ground. The dirt released itself from its iced shield, and his casket was lowered deeper and deeper. This was one of the only moments Jo saw sincere and heart-wrenching tears develop in Emi's eyes. Although she became confused, unaware of whose death and funeral they had attended, she was fully present. She saw her husband, the love of her life, the man with the name that brightened up the sky and her darkest of days, was really dead. He'd vacated her life and all of their lives.

Sonny was Willa's first great loss. Although Dawson had walked away before Sonny had, the loss of Dawson was impossible to compare and far less painful. His disappearance left a fraction of the emptiness in her shell of a body that her grandfather did.

For Willa, to say goodbye to Dawson was a moment both bitter and sweet. She knew he was still out there somewhere enough as he walked around his college campus and made new friends, confident he was both good-looking and charming to find someone to spend the rest of his life with. Eventually, he would love someone so deeply he would come to have little to no recollection of his past relationship with Willa at all, and the two of them would be better off.

When Sonny died, Willa knew he would no longer step foot on the soil of his home, and he would no longer provide Emi with the comfort of love or teach Willa new things on their adventures to the great outdoors. He would never live another life. He was gone.

The man that knew how to live. This was the statement written on a flashy banner in his funeral reception, and it was true. With everybody he encountered, every soul he touched, he made each one feel more alive. Sonny showed people what they were missing and presented them with a path.

"He sure was a man who knew how to live, huh?" Jo asked Willa, then looked up at the unattractive banner and ate the vanilla cake with the same phrase written on its top in yellow frosting.

"Yeah, he was," Willa agreed. Tears formed in both of their eyes. Willa looked around at all the happy faces and the joy they seemed to feel, even though he was gone. It was not the funeral she expected. It was a celebration of the life he lived with no regrets.

———

As they continued to sit at the wooden table in the nursing home, all of them were silent. They thought of possible things they could say and felt awkward in the empty spaces. Willa let out a breath of air, then turned her head slightly to see the western film and if any action ensued. Emi began to speak groggily.

"You know…" Emi finally began, unsure of where the conversation would lead, as she drew Jo and Willa's attention immediately. Both of them perked up in their seats and placed their chins in the center of their palms. They stared at Emi, ready to soak up every word. "You, young lady," She pointed to Willa. "When I was your age, you wouldn't have believed me if I told you what I wanted to be when I grew up."

Willa grew excited as Emi began to reveal her story.

"I wanted to go to the University of Pennsylvania, become a nurse, and marry a doctor, and live in a big house with all of these kids looking just like me running all around."

In all the years that Emi discussed Jo's dreams with her, Jo never heard Emi's childhood dream. "I didn't know you wanted to be a nurse, Ma." Jo smiled, but as Emi looked at her, she seemed to evaporate into thin air and to think of her losses.

"Yes, well. That was before I had a child, you see, Adi? I had this child from an awful man too... just awful." She chuckled.

"Umm..." Jo looked to Willa, but she simply shrugged her shoulders and faced forward. "Who's Adi?"

This statement confused both Willa and Jo. Emi had seemed to forget who Jo was during this conversation, and now she revealed parts of herself and talked in a way she had only done with her old friend.

After all those years, Jo realized why Emi had been too afraid to tell her of her true dream. She had felt too self-conscious to tell her Jo had been part of the reason her greatest hopes in life had seemed to become an impossibility. Even so, Emi never loved her less.

"Well, that is a lovely dream," Jo said as she felt her throat close.

She had dreamed she would become a nurse, marry a doctor, and live in a big house. All she ever expressed to her was one dream. *All I dream is that you, Milo, and your father are happy and healthy, and the four of us continue to show each other love.* And that had come true.

———

The care facility smelled of baked goods and discontent, and each time Jo and Willa left, both of their hearts broke. They did not want to stay in the presence of lost memories for too long, but they also never wanted to say goodbye to Emi and leave her alone.

Just as Jo and Willa reached the exit doors, the same woman who had rolled Emi in to meet them rushed down the hall and called Jo's name.

"Mrs. Woodson... Jo! Can you wait one moment, please!" she said hurriedly.

Jo and Willa came to a halt.

"Hi, what's up?" Jo responded casually. She looked down at what was in the woman's hand. Between her fingers was a small envelope. It was a saddened white and curled at its ends.

"I found this a few days ago with Emi's old belongings, and I knew you were coming today, so I didn't want to forget to give it to you." She stretched her arm to show Jo. "It's addressed to you, and it says it's from Choteau, Montana."

Jo looked at the envelope, confused. From its condition, it seemed to be decades old, but she recognized Emi's handwriting clearly, with her name scribbled in the most effortless curling font.

"Okay, great," Jo said as she grabbed the letter. "Thank you so much."

As they drove away, Willa practiced her predictable habit, in which she gazed out of the window and watched the combination of thick fog and small tears run down the side of the glass. After a while, she noticed they were longer than she expected.

"Where are we going? Home, right?" she asked her mother, but Jo simply shook her head and gave Willa no further information. Jo then took her phone from the cup holder between them and handed it to Willa.

"Play our playlist," Jo demanded with a grin. Willa was pleased to do so. She took the phone from the center and traveled down to a playlist titled *'70s Tunes*, then played the first song.

"Bridge Over Troubled Water" echoed in the car speakers, and Willa and Jo's voices rang with passion and a tinge of sorrow. They loved to see Emi but always felt the pain of losing her each time. It was as if she had already vanished, and they mourned the living.

As they leaned on the outside of the car, mouths open with a combination of surprise and defeat, Willa and Jo looked at a house that once held charm and happiness but now represented surrender. Willa only knew this house briefly, but Jo had grown up here. Now, it was falling apart and was vacant, with no Sander or Woodson or even Grandeur left to fill its empty space. With their heads beside one another, they looked across the way to this pathetic structure, with the smell of wet pavement and sprouting grass that swirled in the breeze.

Jo began to walk across the empty street and sat in the front yard, smothered in small holes and overgrown weeds that desperately wanted to be pulled from their aged soil.

The house held a "for sale" sign. It was the newest thing on the property. They both felt broken as they stared at the old house in which they had developed such fond memories, for Jo an entire childhood, and for Willa, sweet early memories. They wanted to change this fate of selling this house to a stranger but knew it would be too long and too costly to seriously consider.

As Willa trailed behind Jo, she sat next to her and felt the wetness of the grass seep into her light wash jeans. She worried in the back of her mind, it might leave a stain, but she was frozen in place.

"You smell that?" Jo asked, and Willa immediately knew what she meant. The garden in the back of the house, Emi's pride and joy, always protruded a smell of sweetness, and the scent transported Jo and Willa back in time. This was a hobby Emi did not recognize until Jo was moved out, but every time she visited, the earthy smell brought a smile to her face.

"Want to go check it out?" Jo asked.

Willa had already begun to stand up. She circled around the way and looked at the small, cracked windows and the white peeling brick. The gutters overflowed with fallen maple leaves from the autumn weather. They seemed to have tried to wash away with the rain but clogged the gutters in clumps.

They turned the corner and walked through the rusted metal gate. Jo walked through the door and heard the scratch of metal against the rocks and saw pebbles embedded within the grass. As they went through, Jo turned to face Willa. She looked in the direction of the garden in shock.

"What is it?" Jo asked. Then she turned her own head for a brief moment and flashed the same expression as Willa.

They had expected to see Emi's usual garden, with small plants stocked with multicolor peppers and greens, but it was now a place beyond recognition. The size of the garden had doubled. It overflowed with weeds and flowers that leaked from the plywood box. They gave off a heavenly smell, which could have rivaled the most diverse garden or budding forest.

It was incredible. They realized it might look ugly to some, but the blooming flowers spawned great emotion in them. They bound their hands together in a tight hold, rings scraping against one another again, but neither of them paid any mind to the soft clinks.

Three kinds of flowers climbed up the walls of the house: dogwoods, peonies, and sunflowers. These were Emi, Jo, and Willa's favorite flowers in the entire world. They twined together in this garden and brushed against the house where they had so many memories that morphed into one. Neither of them could believe their eyes. They could not decide if someone had done this or if this was purely an act of nature. They could not be sure, but at this moment, they did not care.

"Isn't this the most beautiful thing you have ever seen?" Jo asked lightly.

Willa nodded. "I love this house."

———

They returned to the car, with Jo ready to leave, as Willa looked up through the skylight, to watch the millions of heavy raindrops peck against the glass. The stillness was abnormal from other times they sat in silence. Before they rolled away from the house that contained a part of each of them, Jo paused and admired Willa. She still looked through the glass. There was such wonder on Willa's face that reminded her of a much younger version of her. It was the same Willa who had gone on rides with her sports games or fishing trips with her grandparents.

"Willa?" she asked softly and attempted not to entirely disrupt her tender moment.

Willa looked down at Jo's face with curiosity.

"What is your dream? What do you want most in the world?" Jo asked bluntly and caught Willa by surprise.

Willa slid in her seat a bit further, curled her eyebrows, and used her palms to squish her icy cheeks. "Well, I want

to work in movies and have a family and be loved, I guess...
something like that."

Jo was pleased with her aspirations but unsatisfied.

"What do you mean by *to be loved*?" Jo asked with more
seriousness.

"I want someone to love me... like be married. And hopefully to someone special."

Jo and Willa faced each other now. Willa had an air of
confusion, and Jo had knowledge.

"You know, Willa," Jo smirked. "You don't need someone
special in this world to sweep you off of your feet. You just
need *someone*, even if it's just a friend or family member. I
learned that a long time ago."

Jo could tell from Willa's reaction she did not understand.
She did not mean she should settle or lower her standards,
but she should accept the love she knew she deserved, no
matter who it came from. Knowing there would be someone
by her side, which would disappoint her at times, but she
would love them anyway because they would try to make
her the happiest she could be.

———

It was difficult saying goodbye to that old, white house, with
the knowledge it was probably the last time either of them
would be there to see it in its original form, with small windows, narrow hallways, and Emi's garden that bursts with
floral surprises.

As they drove past the swaying evergreen trees, their ears
picked up the irritating sound of the windshield being blasted
with rain, and Jo had never felt more complete. Since Emi's
diagnosis, her fate had always felt uncertain. She did not

know what lay in store for her and if someday Willa would do the same thing they had done together but for her. She was unable to predict if Willa would visit a familiar face that had no recollection of her, of the mistakes, moments, and memories they all had together once upon a time.

It scared Jo to know one day she might not remember her sweet Willa, her Willie. The girl she had dreamed for so viciously and never expected to be such an example of perfection. She was the flawless combination of everyone in the family she loved, and she gave that love back to her. It is the fear that strikes in the oldest of hearts, and that is the fear of being unloved, forgotten, and dying. It is scary to think about being whisked away to a land proven by no one and possibly unreal, unsure if it presents good or evil or nothing at all. Jo didn't fear that. She only feared forgetting.

As she drove away from her past and on to the future, Jo was tired of walking the path of life with such fear and uncertainty. She did not know where it would lead or how soon it would end, but she drove on that path proudly with her daughter by her side. She considered Willa possibly feared the same thing as her, with the knowledge that one day she might be forgotten or even forget herself.

"Want me to play some music?" Willa asked, which startled Jo from her deepest thoughts.

"Sure," she said, and it was as if they could read each other's minds. As Willa grabbed the phone, she went to all the playlists filled with their combined artistic loves. Nat King Cole's voice rang in Jo's ear's, with the accompaniment of Willa's singing. "Unforgettable."

The song began, and as Willa's voice carried in the air along with his, Jo continued to drive and listen. She felt the aching in her heart burn as she sang. This was Emi's favorite song, which played during every visit in that old house and every holiday. Hearing it made the smell of apple pie and cornbread stuffing fill Jo's senses. It allowed her to recall her mother baking away in the kitchen, with techniques she had learned in her cooking classes, as Sonny danced alongside her. Every moment spent in that house was unforgettable.

Although Emi could not remember her family now, they had been unforgettable to her. All of it was, and it was the same for her family. Despite the challenges they faced and all their differences, as well as moments of pain, questioning, and even fear, they would have never become the people they were destined to be. If Emi had never gotten pregnant with Jo and instead received her life of wealth and education, and whatever else her family could afford, would it have been any better? Her reality was better than her plan could have ever been, despite times of pain. It was unforgettable, Emi was unforgettable, Jo was, and even Willa. It just took time for each of them to see that.

ACKNOWLEDGMENTS

———

First and foremost, I would like to thank my family. Mom and Grandma, thank you for sharing part of your story with me. Mom, thank you for having conversations with me about your family history and constantly checking in to see how I am doing. The rest of my family, you know who you are, thank you for supporting this project and providing genuine and helpful support. It has been such an incredible experience to create something that will reflect part of who we are as women within our family and the struggles and hardships each of us has had to withstand.

Thank you to all my friends and supporters who have stuck by me since the beginning of this journey. Thank you for reaching out to me to show your support and expressing interest in this story. A special thank you to my best friend, Carli Belouskas, for allowing me to share my joys and frustrations with her throughout this all-consuming writing process.

Thank you to all of those who preordered my book and helped me reach my goal in order to publish. This process would not be the same without you. It was so fun connecting with friends old and new during this time in relation to my preorder campaign.

The preorder supporters include; Nivita Chaliki, Megan Berchem, Carlin Kinlow, Colette Ngo, Heiwon Muluwork, Ryan Bodiford, Milli Wijenaike-Bogle, Julia Strand, Rebecca Molik, Gikanga Kamau, Leslie Harper-Miles, Michelle Jaff, Sara Shohoud, Maureen Crow, Linda Myhrvold, Michael Crumby, Helen Buscher, Francesca Dale, Joanna Greenberg, Michelle Gibson, Carol Hartoon, Michelle Lee, Lori Matsukawa, Kendra Hubbell, Loren Wallace, Terri Segars, Sienna Axe, Nikia Washington, Gordon & Dorina McHenry, Mark Wright, Sue Do, Stephanie Bowers, Micheal Greene, Morgan Spillman, Maija Girardi, David Peabody, Rebecca Moe, Lisa Youngblood Hall, Meredith Tall, Lorinda Flikkema, Andrea Westling, Essex Porter, Angela Russell, Dana Frank, Alison Bailey, Justin Riley, Inger Deutsch, Atianah Thomas, Molly Weitzman, Britten Nelson, Mary Harding, David Minehan, Kiara Jackson, Greg Brackett, Aja Estrada, Bryn Bunich, Oliver Wevers, Katherine Wallace, Annette Alling, Stephanie Munduruca, Jolene McCaw, Carli Belouskas, Janice Stowers, Tanya Robinson-Taylor, Joyce Wallace, Eric Koester, Amanda Ferguson.

Lastly, a big thank you to New Degree Press, especially Eric Koester, Brian Bies, Bianca Myrtil, and Ilia Epifanov, for helping me turn this dream into a reality. This book would not exist without you.

NOTE FROM
THE AUTHOR

———

I was originally afraid my story would not be meaningful to its readers and not impact them the way it had impacted me. After all, I've lived through many of these experiences and am far too close to them to truly know how this story will touch others—those who do not know me or my family and the events these stories are inspired by.

The revelation of this story was one I was not in search of, but which presented itself to me. I studied documentary film in college (which I still am, as I'm writing these lines), and one of our assignments required intense focus and research of a family member. So, I interviewed my mother regarding my grandmother who I had grown up with but didn't know much about. Learning of her early life dramas and altering moments, her life I had never known fascinated me, as did my mother's early life, which I learned in the process of this project as well.

My biggest inspiration and desire to tell this story comes from the importance of sharing diverse experiences of not only women but Black women in America through various social structures. Although Willa, Jo, and Emi all are connected through familial relation, they have led entirely different lives as well as had unique challenges and setbacks in their ways. These three characters are loosely inspired by myself, my mother, and my grandmother, and some of the supporting characters resemble those who take part in their stories. In reality, it was a privilege for me to learn more about my family's history. I've learned I didn't know about my mother and grandmother and, when searching deep enough through my own past, even myself.

To read this novel and enjoy it or gain something powerful from it, you do not have to be a Black woman. This story touches on aspects of life anyone can experience and relate to. It not only shows the experience of Black people or women in America but of what it is like to be placed in a difficult situation and not know how to get out or through it. It discusses the importance of the people who stick around you when no one else will and how to continue to make it through when you don't know what to do next or feel as if you are headed in the wrong direction of your life journey. This story is about the importance of family, history, and human connection. Learning more about those you were certain you knew so well but in actuality know little to nothing about.

My hope for this piece is that you are moved and continue to think about this story well after you flip the final page and move on with your life. When closing the book and thinking about what you have just read, I hope it provokes thought about your own life, your own family, and how much or how little you actually know about them. Everyone has a story, and I am excited to share mine with you.